Teacher self-supervision

Why teacher evaluation has failed and what we can do about it

by William Powell and Ochan Kusuma-Powell

A John Catt Publication

First Published 2015

by John Catt Educational Ltd,
12 Deben Mill Business Centre,
Old Maltings Approach,
Melton, Woodbridge IP12 1BL

Tel: +44 (0) 1394 389850
Email: enquiries@johncatt.com
Website: www.johncatt.com

ISBN: 978 1 909717 67 1

Set and designed by John Catt Educational Limited

Printed and bound in Great Britain

Contents

To two strong women who have nurtured our self-direction:
Doreen and Pauline, with heartfelt thanks.

Acknowledgements

We would like to express our thanks to the many people who, knowingly or unknowingly, contributed towards the development of ideas contained in this book. Through meaningful conversations and correspondence, you have enriched our thinking and our lives.

We would first like to thank Art Costa and Bob Garmston, who have long been our mentors, friends and guides in exploring self-directedness. You continue to inspire us with your positive and optimistic outlook on life. We would also like to acknowledge the powerful influence of Cognitive Coaching upon our thinking and thank all those in the Thinking Collaborative community who have supported our self-directed learning journey.

We have been inspired by a number of educational leaders who are actively and deliberately putting teacher self-directed learning on the front burner in order to re-culture their international schools: notably Mary-Lyn Campbell, James Dalziel, Walter Plotkin, Samer Khoury, James MacDonald, Steve Dare, Nick Bowley and Andy Page-Smith.

We would also like to thank Aloha Lavina, a thoughtful school leader and friend whose life journey has recently intersected with our own.

And finally, we would like to thank Kevin Bartlett, former long-time Head of the International School of Brussels and co-developer of the Common Ground Collaborative, an approach to school development that has teacher self-directed learning at its heart. Many of the ideas that appear in this book were explored with Kevin around our kitchen table in Massat. He continues to challenge and stretch our thinking.

Thank you all for sharing your conversations with us.

Bill and Ochan Powell
Massat

Chapter 1

It's all about learning

Over the course of the last 30 years, the authors of this book have worked with a large number of teachers and school leaders in over 50 countries worldwide and the refrain has been virtually unanimous: traditional teacher evaluation is a failed system. It doesn't improve student learning; it is immensely time and energy consuming; and it destroys the culture of trust in schools.

Try a rough-and-ready thought experiment: stand in front of a group of 1000 teachers and ask how many of them are becoming more professional, effective or fulfilled through the use of the present system of teacher evaluation. Our hunch is that virtually no one will say "yes". We have a failed system that isn't working and we need to change it.

Schools are places of learning, and therefore they should be places of high collective intelligence. However, frequently they are not. Arguably the single greatest folly and waste of time in schools is the perpetuation of the failed system of teacher evaluation.

Assuming the mantle of the profession

Historically, teaching has been one of four *professions*; that is, an occupation that required the individual entering it to *profess*, take an oath or tacitly affirm a belief system. The other professions were medicine, the clergy and law. Each profession was traditionally garbed in a gown that signified the mantle of responsibility that the individual had assumed. Each profession had its own values and beliefs and the individual was expected to embrace and adhere to them. It is time that teaching reclaimed the status of a profession. We do that by recognizing, developing and relentlessly insisting upon individual teacher self-directed learning.

We believe that all behavior, including teacher pedagogical behavior in the classroom, is a product of thought and perception (Costa & Garmston, 2002). Adult professional learning engages increasingly complex thought and explores alternative perceptions and as a result influences decision-making and behavior. The learning is even more powerful when it is self-directed; that is, when it is the product of the learner's own drive and motivation, rather than something he or she is compelled into by external forces.

Those who facilitate student learning need to be learners themselves and, as adults, they need to be self-directed. This is nothing less than a reasonable expectation.

Reasonable and unreasonable expectations

The title of this section includes the phrase 'a reasonable expectation', so it is perhaps worthwhile to spend a moment exploring what constitutes an expectation and how we determine whether one is reasonable or not.

Bill is reminded of a time when he was Headmaster of the International School of Kuala Lumpur and a middle school student had been caught cheating on a test. When questioned about his behavior, the young man denied any dishonesty until confronted with irrefutable evidence to the contrary. Bill took the decision that the student needed to spend a couple of days at home to reflect on not only his academic honesty but also how he had repeatedly lied about his behavior to his teacher, the principal and then to Bill.

The following day the student's irate father appeared in Bill's office. He did not deny that his son had cheated on the test, but he felt the consequences were too severe. Bill attempted to explain that the young man had not only cheated but had lied about it. The father's response: "What do you expect? You haul the boy into your office and accuse him of cheating. He's scared out of his mind. So he lies. What do you really expect?"

The father probably intended the final remark as a rhetorical question that would not require an answer. Bill, however, chose to address it directly.

"I expect your son and every other student in this school to tell the truth. Would you really want to send your child to a school where the Headmaster, the principal and teachers expected children to lie?"

A similar question can be framed about teachers: would we really want to send our children to a school in which we expected teachers to be other than self-directed learners?

Expectations are funny things. We don't usually spend a great deal of conscious time developing or refining them and yet they are immensely powerful in determining how we and others may act and behave. The classic study on teacher expectations was undertaken by Harvard researchers Rosenthal and Jacobson (1992) in the 1970s – the so-called Pygmalion Study, out of which came the idea of the self-fulfilling prophecy.

Rosenthal and Jacobson demonstrated that teacher expectations can and do have a profound influence on student achievement. We also know this to be the case with adults. The expectations of school leaders have a powerful influence on teacher behavior and decision-making.

Recent research in neuroscience suggests that when we make accurate predictions we are rewarded with a hit of dopamine – the so-called happy neurotransmitter (Willis, 2014). This makes evolutionary sense. When our ancestors predicted accurately where the edible roots and tubers were located or where the game might congregate, these hunters and gatherers were rewarded not just with food but also with a mild sense of euphoria courtesy of dopamine.

Expectations are a form of prediction. A teacher who expects a student to do well on a high stakes test feels elated when the student does so. Dopamine is at work. That's the good news. Unfortunately there may also be bad news. We suspect that the opposite may also be true. When a teacher has low expectations and the student 'lives down' to them, the teacher may also encounter a hit of dopamine. "See, I told you Eddy wasn't capable of higher level physics."

The traditional teacher evaluation system is riddled with negative expectations about teachers and what motivates them (*eg* looking for what's wrong, seeking minimum competencies). Taken together these assumptions form a pernicious cloud of counterproductive expectations that many teachers will 'live down to'. When they do so, politicians and some school leaders will feel vindicated. Their predications have come true and their dopamine receptors may fire. What may not be immediately apparent is the effect that their low expectations have had. Inadvertently, we may have created a vicious cycle of what Laura Lipton and Bruce Wellman (2012) refer to as 'self-sealing logic'.

Perhaps the most ironic aspect of this cluster of demeaning and counterproductive assumptions is that for the most part both management and teacher labor unions accept it as though it were an indisputable external reality.

So what constitutes a *reasonable* expectation? More often than not, the word 'reasonable' in this context is used to mean 'manageable' or 'do-able'. While we do equate a reasonable expectation with not biting off more than we can chew, we also suggest that in the circumstances of teacher evaluation, a more appropriate definition for the word 'reasonable' may be 'feasible' or 'suitable'. In other words, we need to ask if the expectations we hold are congruent with our desired outcomes. Given what we know about the influence of our expectations, does it make sense to have low and demeaning expectations of teachers and then assume that they will take the initiative and be pro-active in terms of improved instructional performance?

We are reminded of Goethe's adage: 'Treat a man as he is and he will remain as he is. Treat a man as he can and should be and he will become as he can and should be.'

The failure of teacher evaluation systems

Let's take a close look at what many schools have in place. In traditional systems of teacher evaluation the leadership of the school develops or imports a series of published standards or expectations for high quality teaching and the supervisor then determines whether the individual teacher exceeds, meets or does not meet the standards.

The supervisor may employ classroom observations, review of lesson plans, conferencing, analysis of standardized test scores and acceptable yearly progress in order to reach a judgment on the teacher's craft. Teacher evaluations tend to be summative in the sense that they come at intervals at the end of a prescribed period of time and the external judgments are often coupled with rewards (*eg* oral and or written praise, promotion, and, in some cases, merit pay) or punishments (*eg* oral or written criticism, castigation, threats, withholding of incentive pay, and in a some cases contract non-renewal or even dismissal).

Some assumptions about teacher evaluation

Evaluation systems such as the one described in the previous paragraph are present in most schools around the world. These systems are predicated on a number of assumptions and expectations.

Assumptions are important because we all have them and they exert a powerful influence on our behavior and decision-making. However, many – perhaps even most – of our assumptions reside beneath the surface of consciousness and are notoriously resistant to rigorous analysis and exploration.

Let's look at some of the assumptions (we will argue – *faulty* assumptions) that underlie the traditional practices of teacher evaluation.

Assumption 1: External evaluation provides constructive feedback that teachers use to improve the quality of their instruction and therefore enhance student learning.

Comment: The opposite would actually appear to be the case. Research and our own experience suggest that improved pedagogy results from shifts in thinking that are internal to the individual teacher rather than imposed from external sources.

The distressing truth is that no one can compel learning in another person. The teacher cannot force a student to learn any more than a gardener can compel a seed to germinate. The gardener can create the conditions under which the seed is likely to grow. The teacher can create the conditions under which classroom learning is likely just as a principal can develop the environment in which adult learning is likely.

But 'the gates of learning are only opened from within and that motivation to learn or change can not be externally coerced' (Costa, Garmston, & Zimmerman p. xvi, 2014). In chapter three, we will explore ways in which we can support the self-directed learning of our colleagues. We will share research that clearly indicates that external evaluative feedback actually inhibits self-assessment, creates dependency relationships and infantilizes teachers.

School people, teachers and administrators alike, have been conditioned to believe that they are not doing their job unless they are constantly providing external judgments, advice, recommendations and inferential suggestions. Many of us have learned how to disguise these evaluations in leading questions. We, as a profession, have come to associate our identity with that of an evaluator or consultant. This is a very difficult mental model to break. It is often much easier to learn something brand new than it is to unlearn unproductive patterns of interaction.

Perhaps one of the most pervasive faulty assumptions in education (or in any organization for that matter) is the notion that because we have addressed something, we have dealt with it in an effective manner. This often involves confusion between the implementation of strategies and the achievement of goals. For example, in one school that Bill and Ochan visited there was a notable absence of curriculum articulation. When this was broached with the leadership team, the response was that this was indeed something that had been discussed a number of times at senior management meetings. The assumption was that the discussion of the issues (the *implementation of a strategy*) was the same or equivalent to the achievement of a goal.

For administrators, teacher evaluation is often seen as a goal (something that needs to be accomplished – an end unto itself) when in fact it is only the implementation of a strategy. The goal is not teacher evaluation: the goal is enhanced student and teacher learning. There is a shallow and often faulty syllogism at work:

Feedback improves performance.
I have given feedback.
Therefore I have improved performance.

Assumption 2: Student learning can be reduced to a behavioral formula that can be implemented mechanically by the teacher in the classroom. There is one best way to teach and we can evaluate performance accordingly.

Comment: We will argue that the *one thing* that merits the greatest skepticism in education is dogma. In medicine, there may be one best way to undertake a procedure; doctors operate on one patient at a time, success indicators are usually clear, monolithic and simple (the patient gets well), and most subjects are anesthetized.

A classroom of students represents a much more complex and demanding situation. Here we find a multitude of cultures, socio-economic backgrounds, intelligence preferences, personalities and talents. It is folly to think that such diversity could be well served by one best way to teach.

There have been numerous misguided attempts to reduce teaching and learning to a simplistic formula. Glickman, Gordon, and Ross-Gordon (2003) write:

> Effective teaching has been misunderstood and misapplied as a set and sequence of certain teaching behaviors (review previous day's objectives, present objectives, explain, demonstrate, guided practice, check for understanding, *etc*). This explanation of effectiveness is simply untrue (p. 72).

People who think teaching can be reduced to a mechanistic recipe have never facilitated learning in a classroom.

Assumption 3: The methods of industry will work in education. Universal education by definition must be mass-produced and students are the raw material of an educational assembly line.

Comment: The 'factory model' of education is still very much a reality in many schools. The student is perceived as the 'raw material' and the teacher as the assembly line worker. Grouping is age graded and the day is punctuated by rigid schedules that are announced by cacophonous bells. The end product of this mass production is standardized test scores. Most enlightened corporations have abandoned the 'factory model' of thinking. Schools need to follow suit.

Assumption 4: Trusting relationships are nice, but are not essential to high quality learning.

Comment: We will argue that all truly meaningful learning, what we refer to as *transformational learning*, takes place within relationships. Adults, like children, choose from whom they will learn. Most of us will choose to learn from people we have come to trust. Therefore, in our experience trust is a fundamental, non-negotiable element both within the classroom and within the broader school environment.

David Rock (2009) provides insight about how the human brain operates in social circumstances. He has developed the acronym: SCARF to represent the social needs of the brain – Status, Certainty, Autonomy, Relatedness, and Fairness.

Traditional forms of teacher supervision are based upon hierarchical status. More powerful and more influential individuals evaluate the less powerful. Feedback that provides advice and solutions creates what Rock refers to as 'status threats' because it enhances the status of the person providing the feedback and diminishes the status of the recipient. Teacher evaluation systems also serve to undermine teacher autonomy and any sense of social relatedness.

Humans are wired to be social (Rock, 2009, Lieberman, 2013). We have a basic and profound need to feel a sense of relatedness and belonging. Our social needs are just as basic as food, water, and shelter. Without psychological safety (not the same as psychological comfort) our health is threatened and our learning impaired. Trust is critical for high quality learning (Bryk & Schneider, 2002, Tschannen-Moran, 2014).

The brain is highly sensitive to status threat. When status is threatened, social connections are reduced and cortisol is produced increasing stress and *decreasing frontal lobe activity*. The frontal lobes are the venue for deep thinking and learning. Traditional teacher evaluation damages trust and creates the conditions under which meaningful teacher learning is unlikely.

Assumption 5: Teachers will not become better at their craft unless externally coerced to do so by the use of extrinsic rewards and punishments.

Comment: The implication here is that teachers are for the most part complacent and apathetic individuals who are not motivated by internal values and beliefs. In order to achieve the extra mile or value-added, they need to be compelled, forced or manipulated into improvement. This is not the authors' impression of the teaching profession. If it were, we certainly would have homeschooled our own children.

Assumption 6: Teachers need a constant barrage of appreciation and validation.

Comment: This is an unfortunately common and often unexamined assumption in schools – many times perpetuated by teachers themselves and well-meaning administrators. Teachers, like everyone else, need encouragement. But encouragement is not the same as praise.

Encouragement is a self-renewing resource. Instead of having less of it when we use it wisely, we actually have more.

Encouragement reminds us of the Hydra – not the venomous multiple headed serpent that Heracles kills in his Second Labor – but rather the simple microscopic fresh water creature that lives in ponds and weedy lakes. Like encouragement, the Hydra has mastered remarkable self-regenerating ability and does not appear to show the ravages of time, doesn't atrophy and does not die of old age.

Praise can be only an illusion of encouragement and its inflation in schools, whether directed at students or teachers, can be insidious and be injurious to future learning. In a classic study, Mary Budd Rowe (1974) found that elementary students who were frequently praised by their teachers exhibited less perseverance than their peers.

Along with encouragement, teachers need fairness. Actually fairness is one of our most profound social needs (Rock, 2009). The importance of fairness is frequently underestimated and undervalued in schools. Fairness or its absence is perceived as reward or threat. When a teacher believes that s/he has received unfair treatment, there is a strong, negative limbic reaction.

One study showed that physical pain was not re-experienced when remembered, but social pain (being the victim of unfair treatment) can be re-experienced over and over again. On the other hand, when there is a sense of fairness, there is an increase in oxytocin, dopamine and serotonin that support thinking and learning in the prefrontal cortex (Rock, 2009).

Assumption 7: Supervisors know more about high quality teaching and learning than teachers do.

Comment: In our experience, this has not necessarily been the case.

Assumption 8: It is reasonable to expect one principal to supervise 40 or 50 teachers.

Comment: In no other work environment that we know of does the supervision ratio run as high as it does in schools. In most organizations, a supervisor has five to eight direct reports. To expect a principal to meaningfully supervise 40 teachers is folly.

Assumption 9: Accountability trumps responsibility.

Comment: While it may seem *plausible* to hold teachers accountable and require adherence to external standards, plausibility has been called the 'opiate of the intellect'. It often stands in the way of deeper thinking. Accountability can be defined as compliance seeking and is counterproductive to learning. Costa, Garmston and Zimmerman (2014) write that these

> very acts corrupt the system. The overemphasis on compliance consumes valuable time, turns teachers into conforming consumers, and shifts the assessment paradigm further from meaningful authentic measures. (2014 p. 91)

Stiggins and Duke (1988) agree that with all the rhetoric aside, conventional teacher evaluation systems tend to focus on accountability to the virtual exclusion of professional growth.

Accountability is external to self. We are accountable to others, usually individuals or boards of directors that have greater authority than we do. Traditional teacher evaluation systems are based upon the idea of status disparity. The greater authority performs the evaluation upon the lesser authority. Even well-meaning advice can reinforce the perception of superior and inferior status. Rock (2008) writes:

> In most people, the question 'can I offer you some feedback' generates a similar response to hearing fast footsteps behind you at night. Performance reviews often generate status threats, explaining why they are often ineffective in stimulating behavioral change. (p.4)

External emphasis on accountability can lend itself to coercive cultures in which rewards and threats are the primary means of staff and student motivation.

To counter the current obsession with accountability, some of the teacher unions, particularly in the United States, are calling for greater teacher autonomy. The perception appears to be that accountability and autonomy are diametrically opposed. In other words, they are mutually exclusive. The more accountability you have, the less autonomy and *vice versa*. This is a false dichotomy. There is nothing mutually exclusive about accountability and autonomy. The fact is schools must have both.

Accountability and autonomy represent interdependent polarities that must be managed. School leaders must set a non-negotiable expectation that teachers will be actively engaged in their own professional learning. Teachers need to be able to address questions such as: from your observations of colleagues in the classroom, what are some insights that you have had that have influenced your teaching? Or: from your recent professional reading, what are you taking away that has impacted your craft as a teacher?

These are accountability dialogues in which the teacher has an opportunity to explore and reflect on how their autonomous learning is affecting their craft. When accountability and autonomy are managed well the result is a culture of professional responsibility.

Professional responsibility is internal. It is all about being true to our values and beliefs. Responsibility is an essential element in self-direction. We will share research on intrinsic and extrinsic motivation and argue that schools, which are healthy human work communities, actively support the development of an internal sense of responsibility.

Assumptions 10: If you can't measure and quantify something, it doesn't exist – or if it does exist, it's not very important.

Comment: Here is a most unfortunate legacy from the dark ages of behaviorism: if something isn't observable and measurable it doesn't exist. The world according to B F Skinner is a rather simple, grim, manipulative place that is largely inhabited by self-deluded individuals.

In the corporate sector there is an old adage: if you can't measure it, you can't manage it. This assumption has nefariously slipped into education. The most important outcomes in education are manageable and observable, but are extremely difficult, nigh impossible to measure: integrity; perseverance in the face of adversity; courage of convictions; compassion; citizenship; empathy; honesty; enthusiasm for learning *etc*. As usual, Einstein got it right when he said: 'Education is what remains after one has forgotten all that has been learned.'

Assumption 11: Only ineffective teachers need improvement plans.

Comment: The idea here is that if a teacher has reached an acceptable standard of professional performance, there is no need for improvement: the attainment of competency heralds the teacher as a 'finished product'.

This implies that all new and future classroom-learning challenges can be met through the understanding and mastery of a fixed educational canon. In other words, the field of education is static and we can expect nothing worthy, useful or valuable to come out of contemporary or future research and study. How would we respond to this attitude in a medical doctor?

The field of education is changing with lightning speed; schools are changing at a snail's pace. Caine and Caine (2001) capture the irony of the present situation:

> Unfortunately, many countries and cultures are employing a late 20th century political process in an attempt to perfect an early 20th century model of schools, based on 17th century beliefs about how people learn, in order to prepare children for the 21st century. (p.iv)

Schools will not improve by external mandate just as teachers will not improve by external evaluation. The answer to the quandary of improving learning for students lies squarely in improving learning for teachers. As a result, teachers have a sacred obligation to become architects of their own, on-going professional growth.

Throughout this book, we will set out to explode these pervasive myths and suggest in their place some positive and constructive assumptions and congruent practices that in our experience have led to teacher self-directed learning, enhanced teaching and improved student learning.

But first we need to look into the roots of our present thinking. We need to examine where these assumptions have come from – which brings us to Frederick Winslow Taylor's recurrent nightmare.

Frederick W Taylor's recurrent nightmare
Frederick Taylor was an American mechanical engineer who, in the late 19th century, became fascinated, some might say obsessed, with the principles of scientific management and authored a now classic book by the same title. His influence in the early 20th century can hardly be exaggerated. Taylorism, as it became known, had as its primary goal industrial efficiency and increased productivity. Taylor believed that 'work' could be carefully and rigorously analyzed and from that analysis would emerge the *one best way* to do something.

His stopwatch studies at Bethlehem Steel, combined with Frank Gilbreth's work, became known as 'time and motion studies'. The goal was the greatest possible efficiency in production. There was an attractive Newtonian simplicity to Taylor's ideas and he gained a huge following both in the United States and overseas.

However, Taylor's management theories were autocratic, patrician, and ultimately dehumanizing. He believed in a clear separation between mental activity (the domain of management) and action (the job of the factory worker). The worker was to be trained in the *one best way* to undertake his labor and then he was to be obedient, conforming and compliant.

Franklin Bobbitt (1912) introduced Taylor's ideas into education and they have been there ever since – much to the detriment of student and teacher learning. We see the factory influence in schools: the hierarchical structure of authority; the fragmentation of knowledge into subjects; departments; and the division of the day into arbitrary blocks of time.

For the sake of argument, let us concede to Taylor that there may be one best way to undertake a physical task such as shoveling pig iron, but there is certainly not one best way to teach Johnny or Sabrina to read or to nurture critical thinking in Samer or Nishat. What works for Ahmed may be a total failure for Veronica. Student learning is far too complex for such simplistic reductionism.

In fact, we would go further and state that we should be profoundly skeptical of any educational notion that there is *one* right way to do things. We are reminded of the ridiculous, false dichotomy of the Whole Language *vs* Phonemic Awareness debate or the nonsense of pitting conceptual understanding against factual automaticity in primary school mathematics. Journeys into such dogmatic blind alleys waste an enormous amount of time and do considerable damage.

Actually, today's education is in the midst of a renaissance. We have learned more about how the human brain learns in the last two decades than in all the rest of human history put together. Renaissances are exciting and confusing times; new knowledge rapidly becomes available and old paradigms and authorities are challenged. Many have a vested interest in the *status quo* – even when it is not working and producing undesirable results.

Ironically Frederick Winslow Taylor, arguably the father of the 'industrial school', was plagued by a frequently recurring nightmare. He dreamed that he was desperately trying to escape from inside a giant machine (Breitbart, 1981). Taylor's nightmare has become that of the modern school – our desperate need to escape from the assumptions that have kept us bound to the machine model of schooling.

Another faulty assumption emerges from the factory model of schooling: the so-called 'Widget Effect' (Weisberg, Sexton, Mulhern & Keeling, 2009). The Widget Effect describes the tendency of school districts and leaders to assume classroom effectiveness is the same from teacher to teacher. This notion nurtures an environment in which teachers cease to be understood as individual practitioners, but rather are thought of as interchangeable parts or human resources.

> In its denial of teacher individuality (strengths, deficits, passions, knowledge base, emotional intelligence and other idiosyncrasies) it is deeply disrespectful to teachers and in its indifference to instructional effectiveness, it gambles with the lives of students. (p.4)

Based upon Taylorism and the factory model of schools, traditional methods of teacher evaluation are a failed system. They are fragmented, incoherent, counterproductive and ineffective, and yet we persist in expending huge amounts of time, money, labor and energy in trying to make them work. We currently have a coercive system that operates on the belief that teachers will only improve if they are being supervised, manipulated and externally evaluated. We reject this belief because it is self-defeating. It infantilizes teachers and creates dependency relationships. And, most importantly, it damages and ultimately destroys trust.

Emotional engagement in our work

In spring 2014, Gallup released the results of a huge survey of teachers, administrators and schools in the United States entitled *The State of America's Schools*. Unlike some previous studies, the Gallup survey focused on the 'human elements' of teaching and learning, specifically on emotional engagement, relationships, collaboration, hope and trust.

The Gallup report contains the disturbing findings that almost 70% of the American teachers surveyed were not emotionally connected to

20

their workplace and are unlikely to devote much discretionary effort to their work. Emotional connection to our work involves values, mission, identity, a sense of efficacy, optimism and empowerment; in short, purposeful self-direction. The suggestion that over two thirds of American teachers lack it should be a clarion call for a major revision in our thinking about teachers and professional learning.

Self-direction is part of the fabric of being an effective facilitator of learning and we believe that most teachers, irrespective of gender, race or ethnicity, cultural background, previous training or experience will, over time, naturally gravitate towards a self-directed, emotional connection to their work *unless* the system sets up obstacles and barriers that inhibit such growth.

The Gallup study reported two factors that may correlate with the low levels of teacher emotional engagement in the United States. The first is that compared to 14 other occupations, teachers were at the very bottom in saying that their supervisors always create an environment that is trusting and open. We suspect that this may be related to failed and coercive systems of teacher evaluation.

The second factor that may correlate with low levels of teacher emotional engagement in the United States is that teachers were last in comparison to 12 other occupations when it comes to feeling that their opinions counted at work.

The Gallup report also highlights that 40-50% of teachers in the US leave the profession within the first five years. The report attributes this in part to a counter-productive system that actually inhibits teacher development:

> Most young teachers didn't go into the classroom expecting to be highly paid, but neither did they expect that they would be denied the autonomy needed to effectively use their talents. They may also have under-estimated the rarity of opportunities to collaborate with other teachers and administrators. (p.23)

An alternative approach

Rather than teacher evaluation or appraisal (we will use the terms interchangeably) we should be focused on adult learning: professional learning that is self-directed. We believe that the more dynamic and stimulating the adult learning, the more dynamic and stimulating the student learning will be.

In our collective experience in schools, the authors of this book have seen a powerful correlation between adult learning and student learning. We have witnessed first hand the paradigm shift from a culture of control to a culture that actively enables both student and adult learning.

Roland Barth (1990, 2006), retired Harvard professor of education, argues persuasively that the most important ingredient in improving student learning is developing the positive and constructive adult-to-adult learning relationships. He is not merely referring to pleasant conviviality, but rather to rigorous collegiality in which we learn from each other, scrutinize each other's ideas and expect our own ideas to be subject to similar inspection, share leadership, and deliberately build capacity in others and self. The coercive nature of teacher evaluation makes such collegiality extremely unlikely.

From our perspective the outcome of any system of teacher supervision must be teacher self-direction. This is what we claim to want for students: independent critical thinkers who are enthusiastic life-long learners with the capacity for healthy and accurate self-assessment and self-modification. If these are desirable outcomes for students, why would we not want them for teachers as well? By self-direction we mean that the teacher is engaged in self-supervision – self-assessing, setting challenging goals, monitoring progress and reflecting.

The baby and the bathwater

At this point, some readers will be wondering about the thickness of the authors' rose-colored glasses. What ideal and imaginary world have they been living in? The changes they are suggesting fly directly in that face of what most schools are actually practicing.

An assumption here is that *common* practice is *best* practice. There may be a degree of comfort in doing what everyone else is doing, but that in no way insures that it is enlightened, thoughtful or effective.

In order to avoid any misunderstanding, we want to be very clear that ineffective teachers need to be identified as quickly as possible and removed from the classroom. Increasingly, research is highlighting the powerful influence the teacher has on student learning (Haycock, 1998).

The research from United States is clear: a child who has an ineffective teacher two years in a row is subject to irreparable educational harm (Carey, 2004; Sanders & Rivers, 1996).

The stakes are simply too high to tolerate marginal performance in the classroom. Getting rid of teacher evaluation is NOT about lowering standards – or protecting mediocrity from serious and timely scrutiny. We will always need a process for removing teachers from the classroom – most of whom should never have been in the profession in the first place. However, these are a tiny minority of the vast population of committed, intelligent, sensitive and hard working teachers in schools. Why would we design a system for 2% or 3% of the population and impose it on the overwhelming majority?

Professional relationships and adult learning

There tend to be two kinds of challenges that individuals and organizations face: technical and adaptive challenges (Powell & Kusuma-Powell, 2013).

Technical challenges can be resolved by informational learning. An example might be the desire to learn how to use a new piece of technology for classroom instruction. I can read the instruction manual or engage in an online tutorial or ask a colleague for assistance. Once I have acquired the new information and have practiced it, I will have resolved the technical challenge.

Informational learning targets changes in behavior and capabilities (capabilities are clusters of behaviors that have a common intention or outcome). Addressing technical challenges in this fashion is energy and time efficient. We can engage in informational learning from any source – inanimate or animate.

While the source of informational learning needs to have a degree of credibility, we do not need to feel personal trust. We can learn content in a huge university lecture course from a virtually anonymous professor. Accordingly, informational learning does not usually involve a great deal of psychological risk taking. Whenever we are faced with a technical challenge we should apply an informational solution.

However, many of the challenges we face are not technical in nature (Powell & Kusuma-Powell, 2013). This is particularly true in the complex field of teaching and learning. We can and often do come face-to-face with adaptive challenges. These are situations that require us to rethink and refine our assumptions, beliefs, values, mental models and even our identity and sense of mission.

Adaptive challenges are complex and require transformational learning. When we address the truly important outcomes of education – those that are impossible to quantify (compassion, enthusiasm for learning, courage, generosity of spirit, *etc*) – we are entering the realm of transformational learning whether we are dealing with students or colleagues.

Transformational learning takes place in a social setting, almost always with a person or persons who we perceive as trustworthy. It requires psychological safety, but not comfort. Very often our deepest learning emerges from a period of cognitive or emotional discomfort or disequilibrium.

However, psychological safety is a prerequisite for such learning and this often emerges in the catalyst of trusting relationships. Unfortunately traditional teacher evaluation systems destroy the very trust necessary for such transformational learning to take place. In chapters three and four we will further explore how trust is deeply connected to professional learning that has a profound impact on classroom instruction.

When we attempt to address adaptive challenges with technical solutions we often encounter massive resistance, what Harvard psychologist Robert Kegan (Kegan & Lahey, 2009) refers to as 'immunity to change'.

Teacher evaluation undermines classroom effectiveness

The Gallup organization (2014) has studied the characteristics of exceptional teachers for over 40 years and they have identified three common attributes. Exceptionally effective teachers demonstrate:

1. *Internal achievement motivation.* These are teachers who are driven to reach higher levels of mastery and learning. They enjoy setting challenging goals for themselves, monitoring their progress and taking ownership of student achievement.

2. *Orchestration of classroom structure and flexibility.* These are teachers who balance innovation with discipline. They are structured and deliberately organized without sacrificing creativity and playfulness. They are risk-takers who view failure as an opportunity to learn. These teachers are constantly thinking about

new ways to present content and to engage students in learning and discovery.

3. *Strong relationships with students, colleagues and parents.* Highly effective teachers understand that deep and meaningful learning takes place in a social setting characterized by respect and trust. These teachers deliberately set out to build strong learning relationships with their students and colleagues. They do so by supporting others to feel more efficacious and empowered as learners both independently and as a member of a community.

Each of these characteristics depends upon the teacher developing self-direction. They are stifled by traditional systems of teacher evaluation.

A new approach

Sometimes it is easier to change the entire system than it is to tinker and tweak the fringes of an existing system. Given that traditional teacher evaluation has so little to recommend it, we are putting forth a simple (but not simplistic), coherent, common sense alternative that has its roots in what we know about student and adult learning.

We advocate for an approach to teacher professional learning that capitalizes on teacher strengths. We know that we can enhance student learning by focusing on their strengths rather than grinding on their weaknesses. We can do exactly the same with adults. Teachers know their strengths and weaknesses better than anyone else.

However, they are often reluctant to acknowledge the latter because they believe – especially in a climate of external high stakes teacher evaluation – that it will result in others, the supervisors or colleagues, questioning their competency. Nevertheless in school cultures of openness, mutual support and trust, we can not only capitalize on teacher strengths but also use them to improve what they may not be so good at.

As a profession we need to work on the search for goodness. As a general rule, teachers are not skilled at deconstructing and analyzing exemplary teaching and learning. And we have seen researchers and politicians focused primarily on what *isn't* working in education. Lawrence-Lightfoot and Davis (1997) perceive that this

general propensity is magnified in the research on education and schooling, where investigators have been much more vigilant in documenting failure than they have been in describing examples of success. (p. 8)

The relentless scrutiny of failure has four unfortunate and misleading outcomes:

1. We come to view the field (education) solely in terms of what is wrong with it and this myopic perspective can blind us to its promise and potential.

2. A focus on failure (on what isn't going well) can often nurture cynicism, apathy and inaction.

3. Mono-dimensional attention to the negative often results in blaming the victim. 'Rather than a complicated analysis of strengths and vulnerabilities (usually evident in any person, institution, or society), the locus of blame tends to rest on the shoulders of those most victimized and least powerful in defining their identity or shaping their fate.' (Lawrence-Lightfoot & Davis, 1997, p. 9)

The defensiveness that so often accompanies a relentless focus on failure often short cuts the data to wisdom continuum (Powell & Kusuma-Powell, 2013) (See also chapter five) and results in facile and superficial inquiry.

Alex Pentland (2014) would seem to agree. Pentland is director of MIT's Human Dynamics Laboratory and approaches the topic of effective social learning through the analysis of Big Data and through so-called Reality Mining. He writes:

Mathematical models of learning in complex environments suggest that the best strategy for learning is to spend 90% of our efforts on exploration, *ie* finding and *copying others who appear to be doing well.* The remaining 10 % should be spent on individual experimentation and thinking things through. (p. 54)

However, when school people do witness exemplary teaching and learning, we often tend to respond with immediate adulation and subsequent dismissal. We will address this in greater depth in chapter three. We must learn to 'look for goodness', deconstruct it and most importantly learn from it.

This book is based on eight premises that will feature prominently in each of the chapters.

Premise 1: It's all about learning (conceptual understanding, competency building and character development). Learning is scalable. Once we have determined that improving professional practice is all about learning, we need to pay close attention to learning theory. What works in the classroom for students can work effectively for adults.

Think of a fractal (here we borrow a metaphor from our friends at Common Ground Collaborative) – the humble cauliflower. Each pattern is repeated in increasing complexity; the single floret resembles the whole cauliflower. The initial pattern is embedded in the more complicated iterations. This, we believe, is a powerful metaphor for teacher professional learning.

Most approaches to education are linear, input/output models (the industrial school). These models fail to recognize that transformational learning often follows a non-linear path and engages dynamical systems. One promising approach that does understand that learning and leadership are scalable is the Common Ground Collaborative (CGC) currently being developed by Kevin Bartlett and Gordon Eldridge at the International School of Brussels.

When we say that 'learning and leadership' are scalable, we mean that what actually works well for children works equally well for adults. There are common guiding principles that are manifest in high quality learning for children and adults.

For example, current research supports constructivist practices as most brain compatible for children. Accordingly, we have seen classrooms becoming more child centered as the identity of the teachers shifts from the 'sage on the stage' to the 'guide by the side'. Dolcemascolo and Hayes (2015) are correct when they write:

> If educational systems do not align adult learning with best practices for children, it is unlikely that teachers will use those practices in classrooms. (p. 56)

Premise 2: It's all about self-direction. Transformational learning, the kind that really improves teacher practice in the classroom, can't be imposed from the outside. Profound learning happens when individuals own the experience. They become the examiners of their assumptions, beliefs and values and therefore the architects of their professional identity. Motivation comes from within, as does professional fulfillment.

Premise 3: It's all about trust. Trust is one of those concepts that we rarely talk about, except when it is damaged or absent. However, it is a critical feature in any organization that claims to engage in communal learning. Vygotsky (1978) tells us that all learning takes place in a social setting. That social setting is comprised of a series of interlocking and interdependent relationships and it is within those relationships that learning takes place. We will examine both informational and transformational learning and attempt to identify the conditions under which each is likely to occur.

Premise 4: It's all about de-privatized practice. We need to de-privatize and de-compartmentalize our professional practice. We need to negotiate right-to-trespass agreements, to cross frontiers and boundaries, de-mystify our practice and build on classroom success in a systemic manner. We need to capture what teachers do to become self-directed learners and apply this systematically and coherently in our schools.

We also need to examine the role of feedback – the breakfast of champions and losers – in adult professional learning. When handled effectively, feedback can produce remarkably enhanced performance. However, feedback is often casual and lacking in intentionality. The result can be very injurious to relationships and future learning.

Premise 5: It's all about the conversation. Conversation is our primary meaning-making tool. We engage in it regularly, but rarely deconstruct and analyze what makes a 'conversation that truly matters'. In chapter five, we will share some research and observations from our personal experience about transformational conversations and why school leaders need to become more skilled at facilitating them.

Premise 6: It's all about coherence. There is a great deal in education that has become insanely complicated – take curriculum development for example. What teachers want, need and deserve is a simple (but not simplistic) system that is explicitly connected with everything else having at the heart of the pattern a clear definition of learning (Bartlett, 2013).

Premise 7: It's all about differentiation. As we have said before, in learning, one size can never fit all. Differentiation or personalized learning (we will use the terms interchangeably) is the norm in high quality and improving schools. We need to determine the readiness level of the student in the classroom, what Vygotsky (1978) called the 'zone of proximal development (ZPD)', and then pitch the challenge just right. However, when we deal with adult differentiation, the locus of control and responsibility for identifying the ZPD shifts with respect to the level of self-direction the teacher has developed. This will be explored in some depth in chapter seven.

Premise 8: It's all about reclaiming our profession. Somewhere along the line, the teaching profession has permitted its core identity to be hijacked. In many parts of the Western world, teaching is not a respected profession. We have allowed a steady barrage of criticism and mockery to undermine our collective self-confidence and we have become reactive as opposed to pro-active. We have allowed politicians (well meaning and otherwise), the media, and community leaders to dictate our values and beliefs and, to a large extent hold us accountable for decisions that are not our own.

It is not enough to bemoan this present state of affairs. We have allowed it to happen and so are part of the problem. We need now to become part of the solution; our children are at stake. We need to reclaim our profession, one teacher at a time.

Time for a change

There is no question in our minds that many, perhaps most schools, are not nearly reaching their potential to be places of collective learning. We also believe that one of the greatest impediments to realizing this vision is the deleterious effects of traditional systems of teacher evaluation.

Rather than infantilizing teachers, we need to empower them. Costa, Garmston and Zimmerman (2014) write,

> The ultimate purpose of any supervision system must be to support teachers in becoming self-supervising, self-evaluating and self-modifying. (p. xii)

It is indeed time for a change...

References

Barth, R. (1990). *Improving schools from within*. San Francisco: Jossey-Bass.

Barth, R. (2006). Improving relationships within the schoolhouse, *Educational Leadership*, March 2006, Vol. 63, Number 6. Alexandria, VA: Association for Supervision and Curriculum Development.

Barlett, K. (2013) Personal correspondence on the development of the Common Ground Collaborative.

Bobbitt, F. (1912). "The elimination of waste in education", *The Elementary School Teacher*, 13 (6) February, 1912. P. 259-271.

Breitbart, E. (1981). *Clockwork: A documentary film on Taylor and Scientific Management*, available from California Newsreel, P.O. Box 2284, South Burlington, VT. 05407, USA.

Bryk, A. & Schneider, B. (2002) *Trust in schools: A core resource for improvement*, New York: The Russell Sage Foundation.

Caine, G., Caine R., (2001). *The brain, education and the competitive edge*. Lanham, MD: Scarecrow Press.

Carey, K. (2004). The real value of teachers: Using new information about teacher effectiveness to close the achievement gap. *Thinking K–16*, 8(1), 3–42.

Costa, A. & Garmston, R. (2002). *Cognitive Coaching: A foundation for Renaissance schools*. Norwood, MA: Christopher-Gordon Publishers.

Costa, A., Garmston, R., & Zimmerman, D. (2014). *Cognitive Capital: Investing in teacher quality*. New York: Teachers College Press.

Dolcemascolo, M., & Hayes, C. (2015). "What the neurosciences are teaching us about coaching," in *Advanced Cognitive Coaching Learning Guide*. Highlands Ranch, CO: Thinking Collaborative.

Gallup Poll Organization. (2014). *The State of American Schools*.

Glickman, C.D., Gordon, S.P., & Ross-Gordon, J.M. (2003). *Supervision of instruction: A developmental approach*. Boston: Allyn & Bacon.

Haycock, K. (1998). Good Teaching Matters…a lot, *Thinking K-16*, 3 (2), 3-14.

Kegan, R. & Lahey, L. (2009). *Immunity to change: How to overcome it and unlock the potential in yourself and your organization*. Cambridge, MA: Harvard Business School Publishing Corporation.

Lawrence-Lightfoot, S., & Davis, J. (1997). *The art and science of portraiture*. San Francisco: Jossey-Bass Inc.

Lieberman, M. (2013) *Social: Why our brains are wired to connect*, New York: Crown Publishers.

Lipton, L. & Wellman, B. (2012). Seven Qualities of High Performing Groups, presentation at the ASCD Annual Conference, Philadelphia, PA.

Pentland, A. (2014). *Social physics: How good ideas spread – The lessons from a new science*. London: Scribe Publications.

Powell, W. & Kusuma-Powell, O., (2013). *The OIQ Factor: How to raise the organizational intelligence of your school*. Woodbridge, UK: John Catt Educational.

Rock, D. (2008). "SCARF: A brain-based model for collaborating with others", *NeuroLeadership Journal*, 1, 1-9.

Rock, D, (2009) *Your brain at work*, New York, Harper-Collins.

Rosenthal. R., & Jacobsen, L. (1992). *Pygmalion in the classroom: Teacher expectations and pupils' intellectual development* New York: Irvington.

Rowe, M. B. (1974). Relation of wait-time and rewards to the development of language, logic, and fate control: Part II–rewards, *Journal of Research in Science Teaching*, 11(4), 291–308.

Sanders, W. & Rivers, J. (1996). Cumulative and residual effects of teachers *on future student academic achievement*, Knoxville, TN. University of Tennessee Value-Added Research and Assessment Center.

Stiggins, R. & Duke, D. (1988). *Case for commitment to growth: Research on teacher supervision.* New York: State University of New York Press.

Tschannen-Moran, M. (2014) *Trust matters: Leadership for successful schools*, San Francisco, Jossey-Bass

Vygotsky, L.S. (1978). *Mind and society: The development of higher mental processes.* Cambridge, MA: Harvard University Press.

Weisberg, D., Sexton, S., Muhler, J., & Keeling, D. (2009). *The Widget Effect: Our national failure to acknowledge and act on difference in teacher effectiveness*, The New Teacher project.

Willis, J. (2014) What does neuroscience research say about motivation and the brain, *Partnership for 21st Century Skills Blog*, January 13, 2014.

Chapter 2

It's all about
self-directedness

Everything can be taken from a man but one thing: the last of the human freedoms – to choose one's attitude in any given set of circumstances, to choose one's own way.

Viktor Frankl, *Man's Search for Meaning*

Upon surviving imprisonment in Theresienstadt, Auschwitz and Dachau, Viktor Frankl wrote the sentence above about his experience in the Nazi extermination camps. Stripped of everything and everyone who had previously given his life definition, Frankl found meaning in the last of human freedoms – our capacity to control and construct our attitude. It is, arguably, one of the most eloquent and poignant descriptions of self-direction.

Self-direction is choosing one's own way; increasingly becoming the author of who we are coming to be; constructing an internal sense of personal meaningfulness that is founded upon examined beliefs and values. Self-direction is the process by which we continually become. We perceive identity not so much as a static entity, but as a continual process of becoming.

Accordingly, self-direction is a lifelong process of learning; learning that we are not compelled by others to engage in; some might call it discretionary learning. We see it emerging in very young children – we have only to observe young children thoroughly engrossed in playing with Lego blocks to see how focused they are in developing and refining their designs until they achieve something they can be proud of.

Here are two brief stories about self-directed learning in children and young adults.

Colin, the builder

As a young child, Colin enjoyed putting together models, seeing how the whole was made up of the parts. As a pre-teen, he built objects from various bits and pieces that he found close to home, what others might have considered to be junk – a piece of plywood, string, a tree branch, old wagon wheels, whatever he could find. Out of these various bits of other peoples' debris, he made animal cages, go carts and many other imaginative and useful things.

As a teenager, while studying for the International Baccalaureate (IB) Diploma, Colin spent weekends taking apart his car engine bit by bit, putting it back together, and starting all over again until he understood how his car engine worked. If he wasn't working on his car, you could find him at the yacht club doing the same thing with the engine of his small fishing boat, again learning how engines worked.

No one forced him to learn mechanics. No one drilled him on the vocabulary of car engines. No one assessed him on his skills and knowledge. The learning process was entirely self-directed. Colin is now an adult, and while be still enjoys building, he serves professionally as a teacher and school leader.

David, the designer

Even as a very young child, David always loved to draw. When he was still in elementary school, his sisters thought at first that he had copied or traced the cartoon drawings he produced: they were that good. This interest in drawing continued throughout his childhood and into adolescence, but was never seen by others as an important part of his course of study. There was a family presupposition that David was destined to be an engineer. Therefore, he needed math more than drawing or art.

Family aspirations not withstanding, David struggled in his first attempt at university. He perceived his course of study as 'happening to him' rather than something that he had chosen. When his parents asked him what he wanted to study, he quickly replied that he wanted to go into fine arts. This confused his parents, who thought their child should just put more effort into his work in order to achieve a degree in engineering.

David later did achieve a BA in engineering, but that was after he had first achieved a BFA in industrial design. He later went on to earn an MBA from several European universities and then a PhD in chemistry. He realized that, in his field of industrial design, an engineering degree would be relevant and useful. David achieved self-directed learning and was able to transfer it from the arena of his passion (fine arts) to engineering. David is now a senior vice president in charge of research and design for a company that develops home products for kitchen preparation, storage and serving.

Each of us can remember a time in our lives when our interests motivated us to learn something that wasn't required. That 'something', whether it was finding out about dinosaurs, learning to cook, or figuring out how engines worked, may have taken the shape of a hobby or a skill and may even have felt like being at play. McClelland (1967) refers to this inner drive as achievement motivation, how we assess and regulate our performance in pursuit of a goal. When we are self-directed time seems to fly, even when challenges arise. No one needs to insist that we remain thus occupied; or to bribe us or provide a carrot (or stick) to keep us thus engaged. Ready and driven to pursue what is inherently of interest to us, we determine the course of our learning, what we want to do or achieve, and by what means we might get there. In those instances, we are being self-directed.

Both Colin and David developed strengths and talents from their areas of interest. They were goal-oriented and purposeful, taking initiative and personal responsibility for their work and achievements, moving from dependence to autonomy over time.

What is self-directedness?

Man's greatest concern is to know how he shall properly fill his place in the universe and correctly understand what he must be in order to be a man.

Immanuel Kant

At a recent dinner party, a friend, a retired engineer said: "I was always lazy at learning. I never did well in school. But I loved taking things apart and seeing how to fix them together again." Like many people, Alfonso's definition of learning was limited to learning within a school context. He perceived the material involved in learning to be dry, uninteresting, and represented 'work'.

Even when questioned, it was hard for Alfonso to shake the idea that learning was arduous and relegated to schools, whereas 'fun' and 'figuring out' happened elsewhere in his spare time. He couldn't accept that what he did in his leisure, the "taking things apart and putting them together again" was the learning that laid the groundwork for his future career with Siemens, the German multinational engineering and electronics company.

Moreover, Alfonso, an Italian, learned to speak and write fluently in German and English when he was already in his 20s – considered quite late in life for learning or acquiring a second and third language. He became sufficiently proficient in German to read and communicate at a technical level. This did not seem to be an individual who was at all 'lazy at learning', but one who was self-directed in his pursuit of life and living.

Self-directedness and self-directed learning are our capacity to self-regulate and adapt our behavior towards a specific goal. As such, self-directedness is not so much a 'state' of being, where you are or aren't, but more of a process in becoming increasingly self-disciplined and self-confident in the pursuit of an interest or goal.

In other words, it's a journey. In self-directed learning, individuals feel a sense of motivation and autonomy, and persist even in the face of challenges. We assess where we are in an area of interest or learning, decide where we want to go next, and make plans for how to achieve our goals. Our learning is purposeful and intrinsically motivated.

Achievement motivation at four years old

All of us have this capacity. We have only to look at young children at play, avidly and enthusiastically learning as they are engaged, to recognize that self-direction occurs at all ages. We recently visited friends who were taking care of their grandson, Oscar, who was four years old at the time, and learning to swim. Oscar would swim from one grandparent to another, asking the receiving grandparent to stand further away or closer to him in the pool, depending on whether Oscar felt he could swim the distance.

Here was a child who engaged in achievement motivation. He was aware of his own zone of proximal development and was able to set appropriate challenges for himself. He recognized that as he practiced, he increased the distance he could cover in the water. And each time that Oscar was able to increase his distance, he recognized and was proud of his accomplishments. When individuals set an appropriate challenge – manageable, but not too easy – they experience the pride of achievement. This reinforces future motivation.

Rigorous doesn't need to be onerous

Contrary to popular opinion, being self-directed in our learning isn't an easy way out, a laidback way to achieve our goals in life. Unfortunately there are still some teachers who work under the assumption that anxiety and stress are inseparable from intellectual rigor and pursuit of academic excellence (Powell & Kusuma-Powell, 2000). Some actually welcome symptoms of student anxiety as evidence of the high quality program we are delivering. As the medical doctors of the early 19th century were unable to conceive of surgery without physical pain, so our vision of learning may be so limited that intellectual challenge must be wedded to threatening anxiety and at times debilitating stress. It is high time we critically examine this assumption.

In an interview, Alfie Kohn noted:

> A lot of horrible practices are justified in the name of 'rigor' or 'challenge'. People talk about 'rigorous' but often what they really mean is 'onerous', with schools turned into fact factories. This doesn't help kids become critical thinkers or lifelong learners. (in O'Neill and Tell, 1999)

On the contrary, when we strive for self-directed mastery, we put more effort into our work, set more challenging goals and sustain our attention for longer periods of time. We are also more likely to persevere, returning to our learning after facing obstacles on the way, and hold our performance to a higher standard than we might, if either a carrot or stick were to be offered. These are exactly the criteria we would associate with genuine intellectual rigor.

Joseph Campbell (1988) coined the phrase 'following your bliss' and this captures much of the power of self-directed learning. According to

Campbell, following one's bliss isn't merely about doing whatever you like and isn't about doing whatever you are told to do. It is a matter of identifying that pursuit which you are truly passionate about and giving yourself to it with energy and self-discipline.

Self-directedness is all about developing our own strengths and interests, maintaining a sense of optimism and being future-oriented, constantly asking ourselves: who is it that I want to become?

Self-direction and learning how to learn

Many schools embrace the idea that students will actually 'learn how to learn'. In other words students will become self-conscious of their own learning and will come to reflect upon how the process of personal learning works within themselves.

In short, learning how to learn requires students to actually remove themselves from the content coverage rat race and become introspectively metacognitive. We suspect that this is much more likely to occur when the learning is self-directed. We have a hunch that the joy of self-directed learning encourages metacognition in a way that is impossible when learning is coerced or externally directed.

We also wonder about the transfer of self-directed learning. How much did Colin learn about *how to learn* from taking apart car engines? How much did David learn about himself as a learner from the process of drawing? And how much learning to learn did these two young men carry from their childhood hobbies into their adult professions?

Our present approaches to school-based learning, whether for students or teachers, not only don't foster self-direction, but actually serve to undermine it. For example, supervision systems that focus primarily on deficits and correction (by providing advice and solutions) threaten autonomy and status and make self-directed learning increasingly unlikely.

Recent developments in neuroscience research support the efficacy of self-directed learning. Dolcemascolo and Hayes (2015) write:

> In comparing coaching focused on a person's goals to models (of coaching) that were critical, Boyastzis and Jack (Kropko, 2010) used fMRI to illuminate reactions in the brain. When self-directed models

were used, the researchers observed positive emotions and a willingness to be coached. The accuracy of the coachee's perceptions and cognitive functioning increased. More critical coaching processes produced evidence of the opposite, including defensiveness and decreased capacity for visioning and problem solving. Additionally, when the conversations were focused on a person's goals rather than on other's judgments, 5-7 days later, the parts of the brain that are used for perceptual accuracy and emotional openness were activated, even when the subjects were discussing difficult subjects. (p.56)

Coerced learning can cause some of us to lose the enthusiasm for learning that Oscar, Colin and David so clearly demonstrated. Klimek, Ritzenhein and Sullivan (2008) call this the 'dampened energy of an audit compliant culture' (p.51). In many schools, children learn to wait for someone to tell them what they should do next, and then wait for someone to evaluate how well we've done. Consequently, as we grow older, like Alfonso, some students consider learning to be the difficult and boring tasks given to them at school.

Teacher self-directed learning

A review of the literature on self-direction and self-directed learning suggests that these concepts have been studied for some time and applied to the learning of both children as well as adults. Malcolm Knowles (1975), credited with bringing the term into the field of adult learning, describes it as a process

> ...in which individuals take the initiative, with or without the help of others, in diagnosing their learning needs, formulating learning goals, identifying human and material resources for learning, choosing and implementing appropriate learning strategies, and evaluating learning outcomes.

Knowles felt that education in the 20th century had changed so that the purpose of education must now be to develop the skills of inquiry. Interestingly, 'Initiative and Self-Direction' are listed as 21st century skills under student outcomes for 'Life and Career Skills'.

Time for a caveat

We have been looking at self-directedness in isolation from other character traits. In order to function constructively and effectively in a work community, we need to examine how self-directedness interacts with other attitudes and skills. Cloninger (1994) identified self-directedness as one of three character traits, along with cooperativeness and self-transcendence, in his *Temperament and Character Inventory (TCI)*.

Adjectives for self-directedness include being responsible, goal-oriented, purposeful, confident, resourceful, effective in overcoming challenges, and learning from mistakes. People who are self-directed are able to adjust their behavior in pursuit of their goals and encourage self-directedness in others. If these are desirable characteristics to develop in students, they are also essential in teachers and school leaders.

According to Cloninger, the three character traits of self-directedness, cooperativeness and self-transcendence largely influence how we construct meaning of life experiences and profoundly affect our sense of personal and professional well-being.

Cloninger concludes that people with high scores in all three traits (self-directedness, cooperativeness and self-transcendence) tend to be happier on a regular basis.

Interestingly, scores for the character traits of the TCI are said to represent a snapshot of an individual's current state. And, as our character changes over time, as we learn and mature, these scores may also change. What this suggests is a bi-directional effect of experience on character and *vice versa*. In short, character influences our perception of life experiences and those experiences in turn influence the development of character. Accordingly, character traits are malleable, and we can all also develop greater capacities in the areas of self-directedness, cooperativeness and self-transcendence. None of these are fixed.

Costa and Garmston (2002) refer to the tension of being simultaneously an autonomous and self-directed individual and a contributing member of a community that is larger than self as 'holonomy' and see it as a life-long trajectory of increasingly complex meaning making. In their book on Cognitive Coaching (2002), they describe self-directedness as being 'self-managing, self-monitoring, and self-modifying'. While directed towards adults in this instance, Costa and Kallick (2004) have also written about self-directedness as it applies to children.

Being **self-managing** refers to the individual's capacity to control impulses and delay gratification; and to review options in making decisions, rather than rushing into action. It requires time management.

We see self-management in the teacher who deliberately provides wait-time in the classroom, rather than calling on the first hand that is raised. We also see self-management when the teacher, realizing that the lesson s/he has prepared is not going down well in the classroom, is able to re-direct the lesson to accommodate the learning needs of students.

Self-monitoring individuals are metacognitive about their thinking and learning, developing an understanding of the conditions needed for them to learn best. They review and refine their values and beliefs against external reality in an ever-changing world and consider whether their behavior is aligned with who they think they are. We see self-monitoring individuals in the classroom when teachers ask their students for feedback on their instruction and on student learning, and then use the feedback to improve their instruction.

Self-modifying individuals are able to monitor their work and behavior, and are able to adapt their behavior or the project they're working on to accommodate new circumstances or demands. These are individuals who, in the act of production, are able to adjust or alter what they're doing to improve on it, make it better. We see teachers engaged in self-modifying behaviors when they read through a lesson plan and, realizing that some students may have difficulty in learning the concept in the way the teacher had planned, alter the lesson plan to accommodate for the needs of specific students.

In short, being self-directed also means being metacognitive about our own thinking as we make decisions about our learning.

Knowles (1975)	Goleman (1985)	Cloninger (1994)	Deci & Ryan (1999)	Costa & Garmston (2002)	Pink (2009)
Self-directed learning inquiry	Self-regulation (Self-management)	Self-directedness	Intrinsic motivation Self-determination	Self-managing Self-monitoring Self-modifying	Drive: Autonomy Mastery Purpose

Figure 1: the evolution of our lexicon of self-directedness.

Teachers who demonstrate self-directedness are much more likely to demonstrate classroom behavior that is emotionally intelligent (Powell & Kusuma-Powell, 2010). They look for cause and effect relationships between their teaching and their students' learning. This emotional intelligence contributes to the construction of powerful learning relationships with students as well as colleagues. Self-regulation is all about controlling our impulses, particularly disruptive ones, delaying gratification, thinking before acting, and suspending judgment (Goleman, 1985). Individuals with high degrees of self-regulation are regarded as trustworthy, conscientious, open to change, and constantly striving for improvement.

Self-directed teachers are intrinsically motivated (Deci & Ryan, 1999) and self-determined. Such intrinsic motivation drives us to engage in creative problem-solving activities that are inherently pleasing to us. Pink (2009) cites research from the fields of economics, psychology and neuroscience to demonstrate how extrinsic rewards actually inhibit cognitive and creative labor.

We believe that intrinsically motivated teachers are vastly more effective in the classroom than those who must rely on extrinsic rewards. The former are perceived by students to be authentic life-long learners and may have the capacity to inspire. In addition, internally motivated teachers are much more efficacious. Tokuhama-Espinosa (2011) writes about the relationship between teacher self-efficacy and student learning:

> Teacher self-efficacy, or the teacher's belief in him – or herself – to achieve the teaching task, is perceived, rightly or wrongly, and consciously or unconsciously, by students. The students' judgments of how well they think the teacher thinks he or she can fulfill the teaching task impacts the students' motivation to learn. (p.151)

Self-confident, efficacious teachers are perceived as trustworthy stewards of learning by students. The more confidence the students have in the teacher, the more confidence they will develop in their own ability to learn. Tokuhama-Espinosa perceives this as a 'virtuous cycle' in that a positive action stimulates further positive action.

The bottom line

We hope by this point that we have made a strong case for wanting teachers to be self-directed learners, professionals who individually and collective plan, reflect, set challenging goals, monitor their progress and self-modify. In order for individuals to become more and more self-directed they must be engaged in self-assessment. They must be making judgments about their practice and setting meaningful goals according to their perceptions of their strengths and challenges.

In order for meaningful self-assessment to take place, there must be a prevailing culture of trust – which brings us to the subject of the next chapter.

References

Campbell, J. (1998). The Power of the Myth. Video with Bill Moyers, PBS Presentation.

Costa, A. L. & Kallick, B., (2004). Assessment strategies for self-directed learning. Thousand Oaks, CA.: Corwin Press.

Costa, A. & Garmston, R. (2002). Cognitive Coaching: A foundation for renaissance schools; Norwood, MA. Christopher-Gordon Publishers.

Cloninger, R.C. (1994). The temperament and character inventory (TCI): A guide to its development and use. St. Louis, MO: Center for Psychobiology of Personality, Washington University.

Deci, E.L., Vallerand, R.J., Pelletier, L.G., & Ryan, R.M. (1991) Motivation and education: The self-determination perspective. The Educational Psychologist, 26, 325-346.

Dolcemascolo, M., & Hayes, C. (2015). "What the neurosciences are teaching us about coaching," in *Advanced Cognitive Coaching Learning Guide*. Highlands Ranch, CO: Thinking Collaborative.

Frankl, V. (1992). Man's Search for Meaning. Cutchogue, NY: Buccaneer Books.

Goleman, D. (1985). Emotional intelligence: Why it can matter more than IQ. New York: Bantam Books.

Klimek, K.J., Ritzzenhein, E. & Sullivan, K.D. (2008). Generative leadership: Shaping new futures for today's schools. Thousand Oaks, CA: Corwin Press.

Knowles, M. S. (1975). Self-directed learning: A guide for learners and teachers. Englewood Cliffs: Prentice Hall/Cambridge from http://infed.org/mobi/malcolm-knowles-informal-adult-education-self-direction-and-andragogy/ 5/08/14.

Kropko, M. (2010, November 19) Coaching with compassion can 'light up' human thoughts Think Blog, Cleveland, OH.: Case Western Reserve University.

McClelland, D. (1967). The achieving society. New York: the Free Press.

O'Neill, J. & Tell, C. (1999). Why Students Lose When Tougher Standards Win: A Conversation with Alfie Kohn, Educational Leadership, 57 (1) 18-22.

Pink, D. (2009). Drive: The surprising truth about what motivates us. London: Pengiun Books.

Powell,W. & Kusuma-Powell, O. (2000). The pedagogy of pressure, IB World, Autumn 2000.

Powell, W. & Kusuma-Powell, O. (2010). Becoming an emotionally intelligent teacher. Thousand Oaks, CA: Corwin Press.

21stCenturySkills2pager: www.p21.org/storage/documents/1.__p21_framework_2-pager.pdf

Tokuhama-Espinosa, T. (2011) Mind, Brain, and Education Science, New York, New York, W.W. Norton & Co.

Chapter 3

It's all about trust

Talking about trust often makes us feel a little uncomfortable because we don't normally address the subject unless trust has been damaged or is absent. And yet paradoxically, the best time to explore the crucial role of trust in an organization such as a school is when there is a fabric of trust present. In short, trust is a little like air; we don't pay a great deal of attention to it until it's either polluted or absent.

Bill and Ochan visit between 30 and 35 schools during the course of an academic year. We work with teachers and school leaders in a number of professional learning areas. Fortunately, the vast majority of the schools we work with have, to differing degrees, cultures of trust. However, there are a few that do not and the absence of trust is immediately apparent.

When trust is absent, the vacuum is filled with suspicion, anxiety, discomfort, fear, unhealthy competition, and the presumption of negative intentions; rumor, gossip, and innuendo. The absence of trust, particularly over an extended period of time, leads to toxic organizational cultures. And this toxicity is glaringly apparent to outsiders, even if it may be more difficult for those who live with it daily to perceive its negative influence. Anyone who asserts that such a toxic adult-to-adult culture doesn't have an effect on student learning in the classroom is entirely out of touch with reality.

A visit to The Peninsula International School
Several years ago, Ochan and Bill were invited to work in a medium-sized, international school in a large Asian city. The school, let's call

it the Peninsula International School, had recently celebrated its 75th anniversary and the Director, like many of the teachers, had been in place for more than 20 years.

Bill and Ochan sensed something was not right during the campus tour on the first morning. The high school principal, who was leading the tour, repeated oblique apologies for the *anticipated* behavior of the teachers toward the forthcoming professional learning. "They are not bad people individually, but when they get together in a group they can be … well, a bit resistant to change."

This proved to be an understatement. We asked the principal to describe a recent faculty meeting. He admitted that there hadn't been one for a while since the meetings always degenerated into fairly vicious gripe sessions. He described what could only be called rude, aggressive behavior on the part of a few domineering individuals and a nervous and passive acceptance on the part of the remainder, including the school leadership.

He described what S L Young (Huff Post Blog, November 20, 2014) calls 'predatory listening', the need that some individuals have to aggressively interrupt a speaker's communication prematurely. The point of predatory listening is not to understand what the other person is saying, but to score debating points at the expense of the speaker. It often relies on taking items or topics out of context.

The faculty meetings that did take place at the Peninsula International School were punctuated with the frequent use of biting sarcasm, which intimidated the less self-confident and more recently arrived teachers. There was little psychological safety in the school environment and correspondingly little adult learning took place. Those individuals who were open to learning did so in isolation from their colleagues and often in 'secret'.

The need to engage in professional learning was perceived by the Alpha males and females at the Peninsula International School as an admission of weakness. There was a dominant, collective, fixed mindset ('We have excellent examination results. Therefore we are an excellent school. Professional learning should be undertaken by those who are still striving for excellence, not by those who have achieved it.')

Clearly there was a-not-so-subtle tyranny of the *status quo*. Any new idea or possible innovation was seen as a threat to the established and well-regarded order and quickly dismissed with either mockery or patronizing condescension. Change was perceived individually and collectively as an attack on identity. Privately, some teachers spoke of a culture of emotional bullying; others metaphorically threw their hands in the air. Trust simply didn't exist and no one seemed to know what to do about it. Therefore the absence of trust appeared to many to be an immutable and permanent feature of the school.

A visit to the Island International School

While many of the teachers at the Peninsula International School were deeply wedded to the *status quo*, the Island International School was explicitly focused on innovation. For Bill and Ochan it was a curious and eye-opening visit. Everyone they spoke to was fiercely proud of the school and frequently used terms like 'cutting edge' to describe the professional learning culture.

Teachers and school leaders were particularly proud of the school's use of technology. Every latest gadget seemed to be present and in use. In addition, the school had set up a department of instructional coaches who were to stay abreast of recent educational research and support teachers in translating the research into progressive classroom practice. Everyone agreed that this was the prototype of a 21st century school.

First impressions were very positive. However, as the days went by, Bill and Ochan started to hear the use of 'rule words' (what the linguists call 'deontic modal operators'). For example, when describing an assessment in mathematics, a teacher announced that the school didn't permit application questions on tests that required the students to use concepts in 'new and novel' situations. "We aren't allowed to use the phrase 'new and novel', we have to use the term 'unfamiliar'". When asked for clarification, the teacher simply reiterated the 'rule'.

Later when we spoke to English teachers, there seemed to be confusion regarding the definitions that teachers were using with respect to evaluating student achievement as either 'meeting' or 'exceeding' the grade level standard. One teacher explained that she deliberately put 'exceeding' questions on her tests. These were especially designed questions that would stretch the highly capable students and allow them to demonstrate their complex learning. The response from her colleagues was not positive. She was told that the school did not permit such practice because every child should be able to achieve 'exceeding' status. Again the 'rule' seemed to bring collaborative inquiry to a premature close.

As we spent more time in the Island International School, we also became aware of the prevailing climate of praise. It seemed that it was almost impossible for teachers to say anything to or about colleagues or the school without including some statement of positive evaluation. There seemed to be a habitual culture of praise. While this is clearly preferable to a habitual culture of criticism and negativity, it does underscore that the primary mode of meaning making at the Island International School was by way of making judgments.

Praise is, after all, just as much a judgment as criticism. Paradoxically, the Island International School was just as evaluative as the Peninsula International School. Both schools were obsessed with evaluation – they just focused on opposite ends of the judgment spectrum. We also noticed that at the Island International School the absence of praise was often inferred to be criticism. It is our hunch that such a focus on judgment as the primary vehicle for meaning making (whether positive or negative) damages cultures of trust and actually inhibits professional learning.

It is often easier for teachers to see how criticism can contribute to mistrust than to see the same outcome from praise. Nevertheless, this can be the case. When we praise we send the message that we are serving as an evaluator and evaluators can both praise and criticize even if the criticism is unspoken.

On our final day at the Island International School, a social studies teacher sought us out for a private conversation about a dilemma. He had been one of the leaders in the planning of last year's grade wide project based on social change. The entire 9th and 10th grade had been formed into teams. Each team had studied a social problem in the immediate environment and had developed a project that would address it.

The unit of study had taken six weeks and had been showcased to the school community as an example of experiential learning that involved constructivist learning theory and a high degree of student engagement with the ultimate goal of developing truly global citizens. By almost all accounts, the social change project had been an unqualified success. So what was the teacher's dilemma?

He had had several recent conversations with a significant number of students who had participated in the social change project the previous year and had learned that they had unanimously 'hated' it. "I don't understand how we could have overlooked getting feedback from the students themselves. This project was something that all the adults took great pride in. We've really used it to promote the school in our advertising and PR. We pride ourselves on using data to inform instruction and yet we overlooked a primary source of data – the reaction of the students themselves. We may be victims of confirmation bias."

And the dilemma for this teacher was directly related to trust: "I don't want to be the messenger that gets shot bringing the bad news."

For us, both schools, traditional and progressive alike, had trust issues and these issues were an impediment to teacher professional growth.

What does trust taste like?

In most schools, trust is multi-faceted and we recognize it holistically and often intuitively. We see it when colleagues disagree and are yet able to keep the conflict in the cognitive domain and differentiate between assertiveness and aggression. We witness it when colleagues take risks, open themselves to public vulnerability, reasonably secure in the knowledge that their peers will be there to support them.

We hear trust in schools when the skepticism is celebrated and cynicism is scorned. We hear trust when established and novice members of the faculty publically learn together, share new insights and delight in supporting each other's learning. Trust exists in organizations when individuals feel psychologically safe enough to venture out of their cognitive and emotional comfort zones.

Three kinds of social trust

Bryk and Schneider (2002) did their seminal research on trust in schools in the Chicago public school system and they identified three types of social trust.

The first they called 'organic trust'. This is the type of trust that deeply religious people have in their faith. This is not a kind of trust based on prior experience; nor is it a kind of trust that is based on logic. It is a felt trust that transcends experience and reason. Bryk and Schneider did not see 'organic trust' as appropriate in forming the fabric of school culture.

The second kind of social trust that Bryk and Schneider identified they called 'contractual trust'. Contractual trust is the kind of trust that you want to have in the builder who is constructing your new house. You sit with the builder, study the drawings and develop a so-called 'bill of quantities'. This ensures that when your new house is complete you don't have the unpleasant surprise of discovering plastic fixtures in your bathroom when you expected porcelain ones.

Bryk and Schneider did not consider 'contractual trust' to be appropriate in forming the fabric of school culture because the daily professional responsibilities of a teacher are simply too complex to ever be completely and comprehensively laid out in a job description. In a nutshell, this is the Achilles' heel of some of the simplistic accountability movements that we have seen in some national systems of education. The faulty assumption is that we can reduce teaching and learning to a series of replicable behaviors and that when those behaviors are present students will learn. Not only does contractual trust not work in schools, it degrades teaching and teachers and actually serves to undermine, the third and most important kind of social trust in schools: *relational trust*.

Relational trust is not so much about a warm feeling as it is about recognizing our dependency on each other. As a species, humans are perhaps the least likely to survive when the individual is isolated from the group. Hundreds of times each day, we depend on others. This dependency is so well integrated into our daily routines that we may actually cease to be aware of it. For example, when was the last time that you ate in a restaurant and paused to 'trust' that the food handlers had washed their hands before preparing your *salade nicoise*?

Throughout human history collective groups form to achieve outcomes that individuals on their own would be incapable of accomplishing. The work of the group is contingent on recognizing our dependency upon each other. In schools, teachers depend on the principal to create the working conditions that will permit teaching and learning to go on in the classroom and principals depend on teachers to be well prepared for instruction.

There is no question that power discrepancies influence the ease or difficulty with which we establish and maintain trust. It is easier to build a trusting relationship with a colleague than it is with the principal who has greater ascribed authority. Having said that, in most schools no one individual has absolute power and as a result is dependent on others.

A speculative detour into expressions of gratitude

During the holidays, Bill and Ochan very much enjoy spending time with their grandchildren. During a recent visit, Bill noticed that Dylan (aged four) and Sam (aged two) were regularly reminded by their parents to use the so-called magic words of "please" and "thank you" when asking for or receiving something.

When we thought about it further, we realized that we could not think of a language that didn't have specific linguistic expressions of gratitude, or a culture in which conscientious parents didn't drill children in its use.

If, as we believe, this may be a universal feature of our species, what possible evolutionary function might it have?

We wonder if the use of words and phrases like "please" and "thank you" are *aide memoires* for children (and adults) to the fact that we are regularly dependent upon others. These simple words may serve as the glue that binds us into a sense of community in which our survival (physical, economic, social, psychological, etc) is much more likely than if we were separated from the group. From that recognition of dependence, trust can emerge.

Being dependent on others can create a sense of vulnerability and accompanying feelings of anxiety. Trust is when we remain vulnerable, but decrease the associated anxiety. Megan Tschannen-Moran (2004) writes that trust is 'one's willingness to be vulnerable to another based on the confidence that the other is benevolent, honest, open, reliable, and competent' (p. 17).

The negotiation of dependency involves two critical perceptions: our obligations of self and our expectations of others. According to Bryk and Schneider (2002) when these obligations and expectations are clear and mutually understood, the chances for relational trust are dramatically improved.

Bryk and Schneider further enquired into the nature of 'trustworthiness' in schools. They asked: what do we look for in determining whether another person is trustworthy? And what do others look for in us to determine whether we are trustworthy? They found four components of relational trust and called these the criteria for discernment. They include respect, personal regard, competence, and integrity.

Respect

Respect is an interesting word. The base element is 'spect', as in 'spectacle' or 'spectator'. It means 'to see'. The prefix 're' means 'again'. So respect means to see again. In other words, if someone is worthy of respect, they are worthy of a second look.

Respect is often misunderstood to be simply the absence of abrasive, offensive or rude behavior. It is very often not seen as something active that we might actually plan for. How often do teachers ask themselves: how will I consciously demonstrate respect for my students in the forthcoming unit on quadratic equations? Or, when I facilitate the weekly department meeting, how will I actively show respect to my colleagues?

We believe that the foundation of all respectful behavior is authentic and active listening: not simply hearing what the other person has said, but intentionally listening in order to understand. We demonstrate such listening and understanding when we pause and paraphrase. No matter what else we may do, if we do not engage in authentic and active listening, there can be no respect.

Personal regard

Personal regard is behavior that carries the message that I care about another person. In a service occupation such as teaching, this sense of benevolence is highly esteemed. In a school setting, we see personal regard when individuals extend themselves to others in a fashion that is far beyond contractual obligations.

We see this when a teacher gives up his or her lunch hour or Saturday morning in order to support struggling students or when the principal takes a personal interest in a teacher's career advancement – sometimes years after the teacher has left the school.

Competence

Competence is our capacity to achieve desired outcomes. For teachers this would entail the design and execution of interesting and engaging learning experiences for students. For principals, competency is the management of working conditions so that teachers can effectively engage in teaching. It sounds like stating the obvious; however, it is extremely difficult to trust an incompetent principal regardless of all the other wonderful attributes that he or she may possess.

Megan Tschannen-Moran (2004) examined the differences between what we look for in terms of trustworthiness in a principal and a colleague. She found that competence was one of the most vital attributes in developing trust in the principal. However, she also found the professional competence was *not* a particularly strong influence in developing trust between teachers.

This may be the result of the historic isolation of teachers from one another. If we work in isolation, I have no idea of your competence as a teacher; nor does it have a great influence on our relationship. However, as teachers begin to have meaningful collaborative relationships, as teachers design and execute lessons together, as they plan for common assessments, we suspect the competence will play a more and more central role as a criterion for discernment in collegial trust.

Integrity

Integrity is the congruence between our words and our actions. It is the 'walk' that accompanies the 'talk'. It involves honesty and ethical behavior: keeping our promises and following through on actions that we have committed ourselves to. It means allowing our deeply held values and beliefs to be seen by others and aligning our behavior accordingly. It is the opposite of hypocrisy.

The base element in the word 'integrity' is integer, coming from the Latin to mean 'complete' or 'whole'. In this sense, integrity can be perceived as the inner sense of wholeness deriving from qualities such as honesty and consistency of character. We tend to judge that others have integrity when they act in accordance with the values and principles they claim to hold.

Laundry lists and dead birds

For more than 25 years Bill served as a school administrator and like many, perhaps even most, school leaders he started everyday writing a long laundry list of things to do. If Bill had his career to do over again, there would always be one or two of the 'to do' items directly related to developing, maintaining and enhancing a fabric of school trust. He would ask himself: in what ways might I contribute towards building the culture of trust in this school today? There are few outcomes more important for school leadership.

The reason that Bill would put trust items on his list of things to do is that trust often becomes invisible in the busyness of the school day – until, of course, it is damaged or threatened.

Bill is reminded of the time when he was Headmaster of the International School of Kuala Lumpur during the outbreak of Avian Flu. The media was full of stories about possible outbreaks in Malaysia and several poultry farms relatively close to the school had had their birds culled as a precautionary measure. Parents were, understandably, jittery.

At about 4pm one afternoon, the then elementary school principal, Susan Napoliello, called Bill and informed him that a dead bird had been found in the children's playground. Fortunately, the children had already gone home. A protocol for such an eventuality had been developed and Susan and Bill ensured that the area of the playground was cordoned off and was thoroughly scrubbed down with a strong bleach solution.

Susan then asked Bill if parents should be informed. Bill thought that such communication would only serve to make the parent community even more nervous. Everything had been done to ensure the children's safety. Bill and Susan decided not to inform the school community.

Later that evening Bill described the incident to the board of directors, including his decision not to inform the community. A very wise and perceptive board member immediately commented:

> Bill, you have two issues. The first is student safety, which you and Susan seemed to have handled well. The second is community trust. If the parents discover this incident and it doesn't come from you, their anxiety may result in believing that the school is covering something up.

She was absolutely correct. The immediate concerns of student health and safety had blinded Bill to the important issue of developing and maintaining community trust. Bill immediately wrote a letter to the parents about the incident.

Informative and transformative leadership

Power differentials in hierarchical organizations such as schools pose obstacles to trust and so it is the obligation of the individual with the greatest power to assume the greatest responsibility for building and sustaining relationships of trust. So how do principals and other school leaders build cultures of trust?

We suspect that there may be a powerful correlation between the perceived purpose of leadership and the establishment of trust. Leadership is about influencing others and we can do so at either a *surface* or *deep* level.

In some schools the purpose of leadership is to influence subordinate behavior so that it is compliant with established standards or norms. This is *informative leadership* and involves *surface influence*. The leadership tools are the use of power and authority, knowledge intimidation, and external evaluation coupled with a variety of rewards and sanctions.

Even when the interpersonal skills of the principal are excellent, this approach to leadership will be perceived by many as manipulative and coercive. There is always the suspicion lurking in the background of an ulterior motive or a hidden agenda. One of the major problems with informative leadership is that when the pressure for change is removed, the subordinate reverts to his or her previous behavior. The change is often unsustainable because the motivation for it has been external to self.

The purpose of *transformative leadership* is to influence the teachers' deep structures: their assumptions (often held without examination), beliefs, values, and even their perceptions. Highly effective leaders do so by way of inquiry and structured dialogue. They engage in cognitive reframing – not the reframing of others, but the reframing of self.

When school leaders publically deconstruct their own perceptions, they model transformative learning. When school leaders examine their assumptions and the implications in a public forum, they are openly critiquing their frame of reference. They are demonstrating a growth mindset, the humility of a life-long learner, and by example, inviting others to follow in a similar path. Transformative leadership creates the fabric of relational trust and opens the door for teacher self-directed learning.

A deposit in the trust account

Many years ago, after a long and very contentious board meeting at the International School of Tanganyika, Bill asked to speak privately to the chairman of the board. The chairman was a deeply unhappy individual who had an obsessive need to be in control. Bill began the conversation by stating that he thought there might be an issue of trust between them.

The chairman agreed: "Trust must be earned and you haven't earned my trust yet." Nor, in the long run, was the chairman going to provide Bill with that opportunity. The chairman concluded the brief exchange by sharing his pithy understanding of the chairman's job description: "I'm here to control you."

In the West, we frequently use financial metaphors when we talk about trust. We say that trust must 'earned' as though it were the reward or dividend paid for demonstrating desirable behavior. We think of individuals who are untrustworthy as morally *bankrupt*. We talk about building social *capital*. The problem with the metaphor is that it treats trust as a noun when it really should be a verb. Trust is about taking action – extending trusting behaviors.

If trust must be *earned*, the implication is that we must start developing professional relationships from a position of mistrust. The problem with this is that many people never get beyond the clutches of its cynicism. Healthy scepticism is one thing: chronic mistrust, as demonstrated by the chairman of the IST board, is quite another.

Building relational trust

While school leaders have a primary responsibility for building cultures of trust, it is not an exclusive responsibility. There needs to be an expectation that the development of trust is everyone's responsibility. There are a number of ways that we can go about this.

Presume positive intentions: This is when we believe that another person is making the best decisions they can with the information they have available to them at the present moment. This is NOT the naïve, excessive optimism of Pollyanna; nor is it gazing at the world through rose-colored glasses. On the contrary, it is a rigorous and demanding ethic.

Earlier in her career, Ochan served as a learning support specialist and it was occasionally her responsibility to provide parents with the unwelcome news that their child was not learning as they and we had hoped. Some parents handled the information better than others. Some needed time to digest the information.

A few, however, became angry, defensive and aggressive, accusing the child's teachers of poor practice, the school of low standards and finally Ochan, herself, of not providing the required support. At this point, Ochan needed to take a metaphoric walk to the balcony, to detach herself emotionally and gain perspective on the situation. The parent was attempting, although inappropriately, to advocate for his child. He was doing so because he loved his child. This presumption of positive intention, even in the face of hostility, permitted Ochan emotional distance and set the stage for the beginning of a more positive and ultimately trusting relationship.

Suspend judgment: Somewhere in the history of our profession we have collectively come to believe that we are not doing our jobs properly as teachers unless we are making judgments: offering praise and criticism, making recommendations or giving advice. This is an assumption that we need to examine.

When teachers provide feedback to each other, they are very often facile in masking judgments in the form of questions. However, these leading questions fool few and often the recipient feels manipulated.

There are times for evaluation and for giving advice, but judgment shouldn't be our only support function, and, if we want to make trusting relationships our goal, it should probably not be the support function that we constantly default to.

The opportunity of damaged trust

There is a commonly held assumption that trust develops slowly over time, but it can be destroyed (or at least seriously damaged) in an instant. Most of us have had the troubling experience of discovering that someone we believed was trustworthy actually was not. In some cases this may result in one not being prepared to take the trust-risk again for a long time.

However, damaged trust also provides an opportunity for repair AND restored trust can actually become stronger and more resilient. To repair trust requires honesty, empathy, humility and courage. There are four 'As' to the repair of trust:

Apologize: The protagonist needs to apologize to the injured party and the apology needs to be authentic and sincere. Many apologies are not authentic. For example, we commonly hear people say, "I'm sorry you feel that way, but I had no intention of…" The message here is that the injured party has no right to be injured because that was not the intention. This goes nowhere and is ultimately disrespectful.

Accept responsibility: The protagonist needs to assume personal responsibility and not attempt to pass the blame on to others.

Atone: This involves making reparations that are directly linked to the situation that has resulted in the damaged trust.

Amend: Don't repeat the behaviors or the actions that resulted in the damaged trust. Ironically trust can be deeply strengthened when it is appropriately repaired.

And finally, school leaders establish cultures of trust by extending trust *before* it has been earned. It is easy for the cynics to ridicule such behavior as hopelessly naïve. In actual fact, it is the opposite. By extending trust before it was been earned, we set a powerful expectation. We send the message that we have faith in our teachers – their competence, their professionalism and their values. Extending trust wholesale requires considerable courage and occasionally it will backfire, but the cost/benefit ratio shows that time and time again it is worth the effort.

References

Bryk, A. S. & Schneider, B. (2002). Trust in schools: A core resource for improvement. New York: American Sociological Association, Russell Sage Foundation.

Tschannen-Moran, M. (2004). Trust matters: Leadership for successful schools. San Francisco: Jossey-Bass,

Young, S.L. (2004) Blog Post, Nov. 20, 2014.

Chapter 4

It's all about de-privatized practice

Arguably, teaching has been the single most isolated profession. Historically we have defined teaching as a solo act. The unstated assumption has been that an individual teacher, working on his or her own, had all the knowledge, skills, attitudes, emotional intelligence (to say nothing of the internal fortitude) to effectively manage the content acquisition, skill mastery, and intellectual, social and character development of 20 to 30 diverse children without much help or support. It is only quite recently that we have begun to actively question this absurd assumption.

Bill remembers his first year teaching at a public high school north of New York City in the early 1970s. He was visited once during the year by the principal, who made a formal observation and issued a subsequent laudatory evaluation. For the remaining 183 teaching days of the year, Bill was left entirely on his own. No one visited; no one asked to see his lesson plans and, although there were multiple sections of English at each grade level, there was no common planning or assessment.

The times are changing, but many schools are still organized, designed and structured around the idea that teaching is a solitary activity. The evidence of teacher isolation is still plentiful. Many classroom doors are still closed and the small windows in them remain covered with construction paper. Colleagues feel the need to ask permission before entering a classroom where another is teaching.

When another adult enters the classroom, the lesson stops and the teacher asks, "Can I help you?" as though the visitor was trespassing. Principals introduce their observation feedback by thanking the teacher for *allowing* them to visit their classrooms and rigid schedules prohibit teachers from collaborating with colleagues within the school day.

And many teachers have grown accustomed to and to some degree comfortable with the assumption that teaching is a solitary activity. The advantages of teaching as a solo act are fairly easy to describe. First there is a sense of professional safety. No other adult is present in the classroom to observe what is going on and potentially evaluate and criticize my practice. Every teacher has good and bad days. When I am alone with students, I don't have the anxiety of being observed by another adult when I'm not at my best.

The second advantage is expediency. I am the author of my own decisions about content, pedagogy, planning and use of time. I can take shortcuts in planning because I know what I mean. I don't have to explain and justify everything to someone else. I do not have the encumbrance of having to cater to the needs, whims and idiosyncrasies of another adult. Teaching on my own is labor and energy efficient – at least from the teacher's perspective.

Third, there is a sense of emotional security. When I am alone with my students, I know who is in charge. I don't have to worry about stepping on another adult's toes. I don't have to worry about the 'chemistry' not being right and I don't have to tread on eggshells when developing new material. I can simply get on with what I was trained to do: teach.

You will notice, of course, that these advantages are all focused upon the teacher, not on the student. In fact we have a classic case of strategy/goal confusion. The implication is that teaching is somehow a goal in itself (as opposed to a strategy that can be used to achieve the goal of student learning). When teaching is thought of as the goal, the advantages of teacher isolation make sense.

Of course, when the goal becomes student learning, the disadvantages of the autonomous teacher far outweigh any of these supposed advantages.

Teacher professional isolation creates 'egg-crate' schools (Lortie, 1975). Egg crates are very efficient for transporting eggs. They insulate the eggs from knocking into each other and breaking. Egg crates are, however, a dreadful model for schools. Teacher isolation creates fragmented silos, makes mission coherence virtually impossible, suppresses professional learning (Eaker, DuFour & DuFour, 2002) and decreases professional fulfillment. A study by MetLife (2013) stated that teachers who reported being dissatisfied with their jobs were more likely to be located in schools that had seen declines in teacher collaboration.

Let us reiterate one of the major premises of this book: student learning depends on each and every teacher learning, not just at workshops and conferences, but everyday as part and parcel of the work they do. Adult-to-adult professional isolation makes such learning unlikely.

There is increasing evidence that some of the most powerful professional learning takes place within the teacher's work setting, not at conferences or external workshops. However, in many schools teaching takes precedence over teacher learning and there are few opportunities for the classroom to become an environment for adult learning. Richard Elmore (2004) writes:

> The problem (is that) there is almost no opportunity for teachers to engage in continuous and sustained learning about their practices in the settings in which they actually work, observing and being observed by their colleagues in their classrooms and classrooms of other teachers in other schools confronting similar problems. (p. 127)

There are a number of ways that we can work towards de-privatizing teaching practice. Peer coaching, structured instructional rounds, collaborative inquiry and the use of reflection protocols all promote a collective approach. However, teachers are influenced most by the direct observation of the effective practices of other teachers (Reeves, 2008).

If teacher peer observation is such a potential gold mine of professional learning (at little financial cost), why isn't every school exploiting it for all its worth?

We believe the reason that peer observation is not more widespread in schools is that the challenge it presents is not a technical one, but an *adaptive* one. A technical solution would be to provide teachers with time and access to each others' classes. We know from experience that few teachers actually take up the offer. This is because the challenge of peer observation is also an adaptive one. In other words, the challenge calls on us to rethink some of our basic assumptions about teaching and learning, analyze some of our beliefs and values, and perhaps even reframe some of our thoughts about our professional identity. In short, it requires a school re-culturing.

Michael Fullan (2007) understands the magnitude of the challenge:

> The deprivatization of teaching is going to be a lot harder than anyone thought. The deprivatization of teaching represents a change in culture and practice so that it becomes normal for teachers to observe other teachers, to be observed by others… I am not naïve here. I realize that in punitive and otherwise misguided accountability regimes teachers are ill advised to open their classroom doors. But the research also reveals that even when the conditions are more favorable, when implementation strategies are highly supportive that many teachers subtly or in other ways, play the privatization card. (p.1)

Over the course of an almost 40-year career in schools, the authors have seen hundreds of school leaders encourage and exhort teachers to visit each others classroom and observe each other teach. The professional literature is replete with the powerful opportunities that such peer observation holds for professional learning. De-privatized practice is one of the five pillars of professional learning communities (Kruse, Seashore Louis & Bryk, 1994). Many of the school leaders have even gone so far as to provide substitute teachers to enable peer observation or have volunteered to cover the classes themselves. In some cases the school leaders have stated that peer observation is a mandated expectation and have devised peer observations partners.

And yet, in most cases meaningful peer observation simply has not happened. The excuses are legion: "There wasn't enough time"; "I got busy and forgot about it"; "Our schedules clashed"; "My partner didn't seem keen and I didn't want to impose." Each year millions of teachers around the world, most of whom intellectually accept the potential value of peer observation, avoid it like the plague. We are compelled to ask the question why? Why do teachers resist the de-privatization of teaching practice? We believe that there are three reasons and, unless each of them is sufficiently addressed, teaching will remain a closed-door, solitary activity.

The first is that the pervasiveness of evaluation within schools creates an understandable anxiety in the teacher being observed. No matter how often we reiterate that the observation is non-evaluative, the person being observed doesn't believe it. One of the reasons the observed teacher doesn't believe it is because it simply isn't true. Being truly non-evaluative is hard work and requires self-discipline and considerable practice. It does not come naturally to most teachers.

What many teachers think of as the absence of evaluation is simply the avoidance of criticism. So we hear post observation conferences beginning with statements such as: "I really liked the way you integrated the ESL students into the class activity." The rationale may be that such a complimentary conversation starter will serve to get the exchange off on the right foot but what the observer has forgotten is that *praise is a form of evaluation.* The implicit message that the observer is sending is that I am in the role of an evaluator and I am making judgments about your teaching. (The implication is obvious: if I can praise, I can also criticize). Praise serves to undermine the integrity of genuinely non-evaluative observations.

One of the most evident distinctions between a novice and expert observer of classroom instruction is the capacity to withhold judgment (Fink & Markholt, 2011). The ability to refrain from evaluation and stay in the descriptive mode promotes deep shared understanding and, even more importantly, separates the observation from the person being observed. In addition, the skillful observer of classroom instruction needs training and practice in separating observation from perception:

Observation: six of the 15 students were off task for the first ten minutes of the lesson.

Perception: That group of boys in the back of the room was bored.

The former is data; the latter is unsubstantiated inference.

The second reason that teachers resist peer observation is that the observer often feels a considerable degree of discomfort about the process. Often the observers will have no idea what is expected of them and will have received little or no training in professional observation or coaching. Many times there will be no clearly understood structure for the observation, no agreement of what the observer will be looking for or how he or she will gather data.

Frequently there will also not be a clear understanding of what will transpire during the post observation conference. The *observer* may feel considerable anxiety over how and what to present as feedback. One of the most stressful situations that individuals can find themselves in is having to do something and not knowing how to go about it.

There has been a trend in schools to appoint so-called 'instructional coaches'. These are usually master teachers with clearly demonstrated talent and expertise in a specific area – literacy, math or science. However, in many cases the instructional coach has been appointed without any training in coaching and so has considerable content knowledge (about literacy or math) but little process knowledge or skills (about coaching). This is a recipe for stress, anxiety, frustration and failure.

The third reason that teachers avoid peer observation is that in many situations it has produced only superficial learning if any at all. By superficial learning we mean that the observer may walk away from the experience with a new gimmick or trick to try in his or her classroom, a new strategy for bringing closure to a lesson or a new way to manage transitions. The observed teacher may learn little or nothing. The reason for this is that too often the observation *happens* to the observed; he or she is the passive recipient of the process.

We have known for the past 100 years that passive recipients are not active learners. Deep, meaningful learning requires active 'uncoverage' (Wiggins & McTighe, 1998), that is rigorous analysis and probing critical thought on the part of both the observer and the observed.

As we will see when we examine some successful models of peer observation, the leadership of the observation needs to be delineated and shared: the observed teacher leads and controls the content, the observer/coach controls the process. The observed teacher determines the focus of the observation, what specifically will be observed (*eg* teacher use of wait time, questioning techniques, or paraphrasing). The observer/coach and the observed teacher agree in advance how data will be gathered. The observer/coach then structures the reflective process, but the observed teacher analyzes and interprets the data.

This last sentence is crucially important and is worth reiterating: *the teacher who has been observed receives the data from the observer and then analyzes and interprets it.* This analysis and interpretation is what supports self-direction and ultimately self-assessment. We will look at this more closely when we examine the use of data and reflective questioning.

In short, de-privatization of teaching practice is a cultural phenomenon that is most likely to occur in a collaborative, respectful, transparent and inclusive school climate; a climate in which there is trust; and where faculty are committed to being supportive of each other (Mulford, Silins, & Leithwood, 2004).

But now we are going to take a short detour into the often-misunderstood realm of feedback.

Feedback: the breakfast of champions and losers

For more than 75 years, the American breakfast cereal manufacturer Wheaties has advertised their product as the 'breakfast of champions' – clearly trying to forge connections in the consumer's mind between exemplary sports performance and their product. In education, researchers and teachers have also been searching for the 'breakfast of champions' and we have found one; the only down side – and it is a very significant one – is that our 'breakfast' can produce both champions and losers. Feedback can be a double-edged sword.

Recent research (Hattie, 2012; Wiliam, 2012; Wiggins, 2012) underscores how critically important teacher feedback is to student learning. When Hattie (2009) rank ordered the statistical influences on students learning, feedback was number ten out of 134. Feedback to teachers on their practice is equally important to adult learning and a crucial element in self-supervision.

However, researchers Kluger and DeNisi (1996) analyzed 131 carefully constructed studies of teacher feedback and found that while feedback did on average improve student learning, more than 40% of the research studies indicated that feedback actually made student performance worse! Thus the title of this section: Feedback: the breakfast of champions and losers.

While most research on feedback has focused on students and student learning, we believe that the results are scalable. In other words, what is true for student learning is more often than not true for teacher learning. What we can learn about the use of feedback in supporting student learning can also be used to support adult learning.

Dylan Wiliam (2012) points out that there are eight ways that a student can respond to feedback and six of them have a *negative* impact on future learning. Students can respond by changing behavior (increasing* or decreasing effort), by modifying a goal (reducing or increasing* level of challenge), by abandoning the goal (deciding that the goal is too easy or too difficult) or by rejecting the feedback (ignoring it or taking no action). Six out of these eight responses have a *negative* impact on future learning. The positive responses are indicated with an asterisk.

If teacher feedback to students on their learning is problematic, adult-to-adult professional feedback may be even more so. Many schools have excessively affiliative adult cultures that can serve as obstacles to rigorous collaborative discourse. Elisa MacDonald (2011), in an article entitled 'When Nice will not Suffice', refers to these schools as having 'cultures of nice' in which teachers feel inhibited from reaching a level of conversation in which they are challenging each other's thinking. There are several symptoms of excessively affiliative school cultures:

Teachers rarely question each other's beliefs and assumptions.

Teachers will make excuses for less than successful student achievement (blame the assessment, blame the rubric, blame the students – almost anything to avoid analyzing the instruction itself).

Teachers will offer advice, but rarely apply it to themselves.

MacDonald writes, 'If teachers always leave a team meeting only feeling confirmed in what they have been doing, the team has probably never reached rigorous collaborative discourse (p.46).' They have substituted conviviality for meaningful collegiality. Rigorous collaborative discourse flows from the effective management of meaningful feedback.

It is incumbent on teachers to become feedback literate.

Feedback literacy
Simply defined, feedback is information about how someone is doing in his or her efforts to reach a goal. In order for the feedback to be meaningful, the recipient must first understand and accept the goal. In other words, the learning target must be clear and embraced. In terms of student learning in the classroom, the acid test is to ask every student in

the class to individually complete the sentence stem: 'We are learning...' The results can be both surprising and informative.

In terms of adult learning, we would assume that the feedback is focused upon a goal that the teacher has set for him or herself (*eg* 'I want to get better at pacing my lesson with student learning in mind.') This insures that the teacher is the self-directed content leader in the observation/feedback process.

In order for feedback to be both effective and meaningful, the recipient needs to be able to answer three metacognitive questions. They are deceptively simple and yet powerfully reflective: Where am I going? (What is my goal?) Where am I now? (What is my present level of mastery or understanding?) And How can I close the gap? (Chappuis, 2005).

Two flavors of misunderstanding

There are two very common misunderstandings about feedback. The first is that 'grades' constitute useful feedback. Nothing could be further from the truth. Grades tell students nothing specific about how they have performed or what they need to do next in terms of improvement. In fact, more often than not, grades signal to students that the piece of work is finished and can be filed away; no further thought is required. There is no positive correlation between grading and student learning. (We would argue that there is a *negative* correlation.)

If we translate this into the realm of adult learning, 'grades' can be equated with a checklist of teaching standards in which the supervisor ticks a box indicating that the teacher has met the standard, exceeded the standard, or failed to reach the standard. None of this provides the teacher with meaningful feedback that can be used to improve or enhance performance.

The second misunderstanding is that the teacher's responsibility ends with providing feedback and that it is the student's responsibility to use it. Teachers are often much better at providing feedback to students than they are at ensuring that students use it. Giving feedback that isn't acted upon is arguably one of the single most wasteful uses of teacher time.

In the domain of adult learning, feedback is often perceived as an end in itself, a goal rather than a strategy for enhanced instructional practice. Once the feedback has been given, the job of the supervisor is complete.

In short, the acid test of effective feedback is the *response of the recipient*. We will examine in a moment the qualities of feedback that are most likely to influence changes in teacher's classroom behavior.

Everyone, students and adults alike, makes decisions about whom they will learn from. Teachers develop positive relationships with colleagues and informal and formal mentoring takes place. The same thing happens in the classroom. We learn much more effectively and efficiently from people we trust. Feedback is much more likely to be well received from someone we trust.

Feedback also flourishes when we encounter misunderstandings, misconceptions and errors. (When students understand and produce error-free work, feedback is generally ineffective in terms of promoting future learning.) Teachers and school leaders need to create cultures in which errors and misunderstandings are welcome. Failure is not something to hide or be ashamed of. What we want for students, we also want for teachers. We want teachers to be able to talk openly about a lesson that did not go well. We want teachers to reflect critically on an assessment that backfired.

Outside of education there is a clear understanding that creativity and innovation are directly correlated to the degree to which we fail. 'If we are not failing ten times more than we're succeeding, it means that we're not taking enough risks' (Murphy-Hoye, in Sawyer, 2007, p. 109). Keith Sawyer (2007) exhorts us: 'Fail frequently, fail early (recognize failure early and don't throw good money/time after bad) and fail gloriously!' Embracing failure as a learning opportunity is critical, but rarely happens in schools.

Feedback that fosters deep learning needs to focus on errors and not mistakes. What's the difference? Mistakes are the result of a temporary lapse of attention. When we are exhausted or distracted and our mind wanders from the task at hand, we will often make mistakes. Many times, we will catch mistakes ourselves or recognize them quickly when others point them out. We know what we have done wrong and we know how to correct them.

Colleagues shouldn't spend a lot of time giving feedback on mistakes. What we should focus on is errors. Errors result from either a lack of knowledge, a misunderstanding or perhaps an unexamined assumption.

As Fisher and Frey (2012) write: 'Correcting mistakes while failing to address errors can be a costly waste of instructional time' (p.44). We would argue that the same is true in respect of adult learning.

Distinguishing between 'mistakes' and 'errors' requires the teacher to engage in cognitive empathy – projecting him or herself into the mind of the novice learner – literally stepping into the shoes of misunderstanding. This can require rigorous critical thinking on the part of the teacher. Cognitive empathy is critically important when an experienced teacher is mentoring a beginning teacher.

Five kinds of feedback

Drawing on the work of Costa and Garmston (2013) and Rattan, Good and Dweck (2012), we have identified five kinds of feedback. Each has a different influence upon the recipient and each has a different effect on future self-directed learning. We have organized them in order of their effectiveness in supporting self-directed teacher learning. These are the types of feedback that the observer might give to the teacher who has been observed.

Non-judgmental data coupled with reflective questions: This is the most powerful feedback in terms of supporting self-directed learning on the part of a colleague. During the pre-observation conference, the teacher to be observed identifies the specific focus of the observation and then the observing coach and the teachers agree on how the data will be gathered. In the post observation, reflecting conference, the coach provides the data in a non-judgmental fashion and asks reflective questions.

For example, "During the lesson you moved from one part of the room to another, each time you presented students with a different content chunk. What were some of the factors that might have influenced your decisions about when and where to move?"

The data is neutral and non-judgmental. The reflective question employs plural forms ('what factors'), exploratory language ('*might* have influenced') and has positive presuppositions embedded within it (the assumption that the teacher's behavior was driven by deliberate decision making).

The observed teacher is tasked with the analysis and interpretation of the data. This may be counterintuitive, especially to teachers who have come to assume that feedback must be judgmental. However, if the observed teacher is going to take the lead in respect to the content of the conversation, he or she must engage in the critical analysis. The observed teacher searches for patterns, makes comparisons, identifies causal relationships, draws inferences, and generally makes meaning from the data. As a result, he or she also comes to engage in self-assessment and arrives at his or her own judgments and personal recommendations.

Because the observed teacher is in charge of the interpretation, he or she comes to own the ensuing insights, connections or new learnings. This ownership makes it much more likely that the teacher will act upon the new insight; much more likely that the teacher will have the energy for classroom implementation.

Inferences and interpretations: These have very limited influence on supporting self-directed learning because the inferences are often evaluatory and the evidence for the praise or criticism is often absent. As a result the inference may come across merely as the observer's opinion unsubstantiated by data. Interpretations by the external observer deny the opportunity for the teacher to make his or her own meaning. This is especially true when the observer imposes statements of causality.

Some examples of inferences and interpretations:

The sequencing of your lesson really enhanced student learning.

The examples that you provided support concept attainment.

The students were having fun while they were learning.

Personal observations, preferences and opinions: When the opinions are positive ("I really liked the way you introduced fractions"), they may serve to develop rapport and conviviality, supporting what MacDonald (2011) calls the 'culture of nice'. They are, however, very unlikely to support the deep thinking of the other person or result in rigorous collaborative discourse. When the opinions are negative we are in the domain of judgments. (See below.)

Judgments and evaluations: For many teachers, the construction of judgments has become habitual and it is a difficult habit to break. The observer may believe that making such evaluative statements – either positive or negative – is helpful and reinforcing; however, the opposite appears to be the case. Costa and Garmston (2013) write 'Evaluative feedback makes the smallest contribution to learning or behavioral change' (p.2).

When a judgment is made, no matter whether it is positive or negative, the message is sent that the observer is the arbitrator of quality. This serves to undermine self-directed learning. Positive judgments create a temporary pleasant feeling in the recipient, but also decreases the capacity of the individual to create his or her own meaning and, because praise is a form of judgment, actually reinforces the corrosive nature of external evaluation. Negative judgments foster mistrust and fear. Carol Sanford's research (1995) suggests that external evaluative feedback inhibits accurate self-assessment. It creates dependency relationships and infantilizes teachers.

One common occurrence is when colleagues attempt to disguise criticism in the form of a question (*eg* "How might student learning have been enhanced if you had checked for understanding?" Or "What are your thoughts about sharing the learning outcome of the lesson with students?") The recipient of such questions immediately recognizes that they are not real questions, but rather lame attempts to sugar-coat criticism. Trust is damaged.

Comfort-oriented feedback: Perhaps the most insidious form of feedback is comfort-oriented feedback in which, in an effort to momentarily assuage disappointment, the provider of feedback attributes the cause of the failure to something outside the control of the individual concerned.

In the case of students this can be when we attribute difficulties in achievement to an absence of natural talent or a specific type of intelligence. We hear comfort-oriented feedback when a teacher or parent says: "You are a good person with many talents, but not everyone can be good in math." The cause of the disappointing performance is assumed to be outside the control of the individual concerned who therefore cannot be held responsible for it.

Four recent studies indicate that comforting students who struggle in math de-motivates them and decreases the number of students pursuing math-related subjects (Rattan, Good & Dweck, 2012). The studies explored whether holding a fixed theory of ability – that is, believing that ability is innate and unchanging – leads teachers and parents not only to comfort students for their perceived low ability following failure, but also to use practices that actually encourage student longterm low achievement.

As we have written earlier, adults continue to grow cognitively and emotionally throughout their lifetimes. It is critically important for schools to embrace a developmental stance towards teacher growth: to assume a Growth Mindset (Dweck, 2007) for teachers. This is not the prevailing belief, at least in the United States where, according to a recent Gallup Study (2014) 70% of Americans say that a person's ability to teach comes from natural talent. Teachers have little or no control over natural talent. It is not something that can be developed or enhanced; it is something the individual was born with. This faulty assumption represents a Fixed Mindset (Dweck, 2007) and constitutes a major attitudinal impediment to instructional improvement.

Comfort-oriented feedback creates Fixed Mindsets in which teachers come to believe that the master craftsman in the class is born rather than developed over time. We hear comfort-oriented feedback between colleagues, when a teacher says: "I had that class last year and I couldn't do any better with them" or "I completely understand the frustration you're feeling towards Harold. I don't understand why the administration admits kids with problems like his. We're just not equipped to deal with them."

Students who received comfort-oriented feedback often assumed the teacher had low expectations for what they might accomplish. This can result in lower student engagement in their learning even when the feedback included a complimentary opening clause. For example, "I admire your tenacity, but it may be that you just don't have an ear for learning a foreign language."

The report concluded that teachers and parents who provided comfort-oriented feedback might have done so with the best of intentions. These may be exceptionally kind and empathetic teachers, but they inadvertently disable students from future learning. This is also true with respect to teacher-to-teacher feedback. In excessively affiliative schools, comfort-oriented feedback may be used with the best of intentions to provide momentary solace for a teacher who has encountered difficulties often at the expense of meaningful future learning.

De-privatized practice in middle school social studies

Several years ago, Bill was called into a large European international school to demonstrate non-judgmental classroom observation and subsequent reflective Cognitive Coaching. He asked for volunteers to work with him and a very experienced middle school social studies teacher invited him to observe her in her classroom.

Before the actual observation, Bill met with the teacher and asked her what specifically she would like him to observe. After several moments of silence, she said that she would like Bill to listen to her questions. She explained that she would set the class some work and then call individual students up for private conferences. She would be asking the students questions about the unit of study on the American Civil War that they were just completing. Bill suggested that he would script her questions as a means of collecting data and she agreed that this would be an appropriate approach.

In the classroom Bill positioned himself next to the teacher. As the students were called up to her desk, Bill wrote the name of the student and recorded the teacher's question verbatim. He did not record the student responses. At the end of the lesson, after the students had been dismissed, Bill asked the teacher about her impressions in respect of her questioning.

She thought it was "just fine." She had managed to elicit some thoughtful responses and had got through most of the students in the classroom. Bill then asked if she would like to see the data. Bill handed the script of the questions to the teacher and asked her to see if any patterns were emerging. She read them in silence for several minutes and Bill became aware that the blood was draining from her face. Finally she announced: "This is not the teacher I want to be."

Bill asked what she meant and she responded by saying that there was indeed a pattern – one that she wasn't happy with. All of the students she perceived to be highly capable received open-ended questions that required critical analysis, comparison or evaluation; some were even encouraged to engage in metacognition about their learning.

However, the students who she perceived to be less capable received primarily closed questions that relied on recall. She commented that she would never have been aware of the pattern had it not been for the data. She had been completely unaware of the influence that her expectations of specific students had on the questions she asked them.

Note that the teacher's initial response was at the level of identity: "This is not the teacher I want to be." She was engaged in transformational learning that related directly to her values, beliefs and assumptions.

Part of the power of this observation and subsequent conversation came from the honesty, self-confidence and internal values of the teacher. However, these were liberated by the fact that she was the one who analyzed the data (Bill didn't know the students and therefore could not have done so); she was the one who identified the pattern and made meaning from it. She was also the one who would use her new insight in future lesson planning.

The egalitarian paradox

Teaching is an odd profession and the authors of this book have spent thousand of hours trying to explain the culture of schools to boards of trustees more familiar with corporate environments. As a generalization, teachers tend to value an egalitarian culture that affirms social, political and economic equality for all colleagues. For this reason (among many others) many teachers oppose merit pay and heads of department or team leaders may not want anything to do with the supervision of colleagues.

This produces an interesting paradox when schools employ instructional coaches. For the most part these instructional coaches are master teachers with considerable expertise. However, they have a non-supervisory relationship with colleagues and they recognize that their ability to influence their colleague's instructional behavior will depend on developing a trusting relationship.

The coaches will also often understand that power disparity has a negative influence on trust. It is easier to develop a trusting relationship with a colleague than with someone in an ascribed position of authority such as the principal or someone with recognized expertise (knowledge authority).

We have observed numerous occasions in which the instructional coach will actually de-emphasize their status as an expert in an attempt to establish egalitarian trust. The coach may actually say something along the lines: "I'm not the expert here and I certainly don't have all the answers, but maybe together we can make sense out of the situation." The statement may make the coach sound humble and approachable and yet it may inadvertently undermine the work of improving instruction.

Mangin and Stoelinga (2011) state that instructional coaches who describe themselves as non-experts may unintentionally devolve their work and become a less desirable resource. Who wants to seek advice or support from someone who, by his or her own admission, doesn't have expertise? It would be like taking your car in to be repaired by a kindly librarian.

The research lesson model

A particularly effective way of de-privatizing teaching practice is to engage an instructional team in the collective planning, observation and reflection on a lesson, what Hattie (2009) refers to as 'Micro-Teaching' or what the Japanese refer to as a 'Lesson Study Model' or label 'Research Lesson Model'.

The model originated in Japan, but had its roots in American pedagogical theory. It is credited with dramatic success in improving the Japanese elementary school system, transforming it from teacher-centered instruction to student centered learning and from the rote memory of algorithms to deep conceptual understanding.

Akihiko Takahashi, one of the primary proponents of *juyokenkyo* (roughly translated as the Lesson Study Model) was profoundly influenced by the work in the 1980s of the US-based National Council of Teachers of Mathematics. However years later, when he came to actually teach in America, he was surprised to find how rarely teachers discussed their teaching methods.

> A year after he got to Chicago, he went to a one-day conference of teachers and mathematicians and was perplexed by the fact that the gathering occurred only twice a year. In Japan, meetings between math-education professors and teachers happened as a matter of course, even before the new American ideas arrived. More distressing to Takahashi was that American teachers had almost no opportunities to watch one another teach (Green, 2014).

The success of the Research Lesson Model is in part attributable to the fact that it is embedded in the practical context of the classroom; it focuses on meaningful and relevant problems and is collective in approach. The model uses concrete practical materials to focus on meaningful problems, takes explicit account of the context of the classroom and the experiences of teachers, and provides on-site teacher support within a collegial framework.

What we know to be true for students also applies for the professional learning of adults. Like students, teachers learn best by doing (by actually teaching) and building their own understanding rather than being told.

The Research Lesson Model follows a three-step procedure as follows:

1. The instructional team engages in collaborative planning in order to develop meaningful long term learning goals for students. (These may be framed as big ideas, enduring understandings or essential questions.) The team then identifies the success indicators, what will students be doing or saying that will provide evidence that they have achieved deep understanding or mastery. Once the team has a clear indication of what student learning success will look like, they collaboratively design the classroom learning experiences that are aligned to the learning outcomes.

2. One or two volunteers conduct the lesson while the remainder of the team observes the student learning, engagement and behaviors.

3. The team holds a debriefing session to analyze, reflect on and revise the lesson plan. Because the lesson has been designed collaboratively, the team owns the plan collectively and has a vested interest in its success and refinement. In the debriefing session the team comes together to review and analyze the data, make sense and meaning of educational ideas and theories, challenges individual and shared assumptions about teaching and learning, and not the least importantly, enjoy collaborative support amongst colleagues. (Takahashi & Yoshida, 2004)

The reflection that occurs during the debriefing session encourages participants to see teaching and learning from different perspectives, perhaps most importantly through the eyes of the student learners.

Research lessons help you see your teaching from various points of view... A lesson is like a swiftly flowing river; when you're teaching you must make judgments instantly. When you do a research lesson, your colleagues write down your words and the students' words. Your real profile as a teacher is revealed to you for the first time." (Teacher cited in Lewis & Tsuchida, 1998, p. 15)

Research Lessons de-privatize teaching practice in a number of ways. They build a common and shared language for professional discourse and frameworks for collaborative analysis. In addition, Research Lessons strengthen professional communities by developing, practicing and reinforcing the norms of both inquiry and collegial accountability. They build an ethos of collegial support and cultures of trust.

Endgame: optimizing teacher talent

One of the enormous benefits of de-privatizing teaching practice is that we can bring to light previously hidden teaching talent. Unlike the media's current feeding frenzy over not-yet-widely recognized talent (the TV reality shows are legion), schools are not places in which talent is frequently or widely recognized. In our striving to be egalitarian, there appears to have emerged a tacit conspiracy for teachers to hide their lamps under a bushel. Costa, Garmston and Zimmerman (2014) write:

> While our media rich culture places high value on talent, the irony is that in most schools talent is underrated and often teachers remain silent about their own beliefs about talent. (p. 99)

Why is this? Why don't more master teachers publicly display their talents before their colleagues so that others can learn from them? There may be a number of reasons that teacher talent remains largely hidden.

First of all, there have been a considerable number of educational reforms, particularly in the United States, that have not sought to identify and nurture teacher talent, but to make it less relevant (Gallup, 2014). The idea was that through a standardization of teaching practice, a reduction in variability of pedagogy, schools could bring even the least effective teachers up to a minimal standard. This approach fundamentally de-valued the role of teacher talent in the classroom.

Second, there is the propensity of teachers to be egalitarian. Some teachers may perceive the public recognition of expertise as carrying with it an assumed and unwelcome sense of responsibility and authority. And there may also be anxiety over uninvited comparisons with colleagues. A person on a pedestal makes a much easier target than one who hides his or her lamp under a bushel.

Third, there is the pernicious effect of punitive and often capricious teacher evaluation system. In 1957, Mao Zedong announced: 'Letting a hundred flowers blossom and a hundred schools of thought contend is the policy for promoting the arts and sciences.' We may never know whether this was a deliberate trap to flush out intellectual dissidents by encouraging them to go public with their criticism of the regime. However, many of those who put forward views that were unwelcome to Mao were executed. The critics of Mao have reframed his announcement: 'When the snakes poke their heads out of the ground, cut them off.'

We may see a not too dissimilar phenomenon in some schools. Supervisors who conduct teacher evaluations may know less about teaching and learning than those they are supervising. They may use simplistic behavioral checklists they don't fully understand and often assume that if they haven't found something wrong during an observation, they haven't done their job properly.

Some supervisors may work an evaluation algorithm that misses the big picture of student learning and focuses on minor or even trivial matters. These evaluations are quickly perceived by teachers to be highly suspect, professionally meaningless and worse still capricious. When the external teacher evaluation system is not reasonably predictable, a climate of mistrust and fear will pervade. In such cultures, the message is clear: Keep your head down and try not to be noticed. This can be a huge barrier to teachers sharing expertise and talents.

We need to create school cultures where teacher talents are publicly celebrated. Costa, Garmston and Zimmerman (2014) write: 'Areas of expertise and talent should be identified, fostered, nurtured and made public. Teachers should find themselves regularly consulting with peers in areas of expertise.' (p.99)

We believe that the greatest educational resources that teachers have are their professional colleagues. Unfortunately this is still a much under-utilized resource in schools. When schools deliberately start down the path of de-privatizing teaching practice, we begin to bring these talents out of the closet so that others can learn from them. In short, we optimize professional talent; the individual strengthens the system.

References:

Chappuis, J. (2005). 'Helping Students to Understand Assessment', Educational Leadership, 63(3), 39 - 43.

Costa, A. & Garmston, R. (2013). 'Supporting Self-Directed Learners: Five forms of feedback', ASCD Express, June 6, 2013, 8(18).

Costa A., Garmston, R. & Zimmerman, D. (2014). Cognitive capital: Investing in teacher quality. New York: Teachers College Press.

Dweck, C. (2007). Mindset: The new psychology of success. New York: Random House.

Eaker, R. DuFour R., & DuFour R. (2002). Getting started: Reculturing schools to become professional learning communities. IN: Solution Tree.

Elmore, R. (2004). School reform from the inside out. Cambridge MA: Harvard University Press.

Fink. S. & Markholt, A. (2011). Leading for Instructional Improvement: How successful leaders develop teaching and Learning Expertise. San Francisco: John Wiley & Sons.

Fisher, D. & Frey, N. (2012). 'Making Time for Feedback', Educational Leadership, 70(1), 42 – 47.

Fullan, M. (2007) 'Change the Terms for Teacher Learning', National Staff Development Council, Vol. 28, No. 3 Summer, 2007.

Gallup Poll Organization (2014), The State of American Schools.

Green, E. (2014) 'Why do Americans Stink at Math', New York Times Magazine, July 23, 2014.

Hattie, J. (2012). 'Know Thy Impact', Educational Leadership, 70(1), 18-23.

Hattie, J. (2009). Visible learning: A synthesis of over 800 meta-analyses relating to achievement. New York: Routledge.

Kluger, A. N., & DeNisi, A. (1996). 'The effects of feedback interventions on performance: A historical review, a meta-analysis, and a preliminary feedback intervention theory.' Psychological Bulletin, 119(2), 254-284.

Kruse, S., Seashore Louis, K. & Bryk, A. (1994) 'Building Professional Communities in schools', Issues in School Restructuring, Issue Report 6, Spring, 1994.

Lewis, C. & Tsuchida, I. (1998). 'A lesson is like a swiftly flowing river: Research lessons and the improvement of Japanese education', American Educator, Winter, 14-17 & 50-52.

Lortie, D. (1975). Schoolteacher: A sociological review. Chicago: Chicago University Press.

MacDonald, E. (2011). 'When nice won't suffice', Learning Forward, June 2011, Vol 32, No. 3.

Mangin, M. & Stoelinga, S. (2011). 'Peer? Expert? Teacher Leaders struggle to gain trust while establishing their expertise', Journal of Staff Development 32(3) p. 48-51.

Metlife, Inc. (2013). The Metlife Survey of the American Teacher: Challenges for school leadership, New York, N.Y. Metlife.

Mulford, W., Silins, H., & Leithwood, K. (2004). Educational leadership for organizational learning and improved school outcomes, Norwell MA. Kluwer Academic Publishers.

Rattan, A. Good, C. & Dweck, C. (2012). 'It's OK—Not Everyone can be Good at Math': Instructors with an entity theory comfort (and demotivate) students, Journal of Experimental Social Psychology, (2012), doi: 10.1016/j.jesp.2011.12.012.

Reeves, D. (2008). Reframing teacher leadership to improve your school, Alexandria, VA: Association for Supervision and Curriculum Development.

Sanford, C. (1995). Myths of organizational effectiveness at work. Battle Ground, WA: Springfield.

Sawyer, K. (2007). Group Genius: The Creative Power of Collaboration. New York: Basic Books.

Takahashi, A. & Yoshida, M. (2004). 'Ideas for establishing Lesson Study Communities', Teaching Children Mathematics, (May) 436-443.

Wiggins, G. (2012). 'Seven Keys to Effective Feedback', Educational Leadership, 70(1), 11-16.

Wiggins, G. & McTighe, J. (1998). Understanding by Design. Alexandria, VA: Association for Supervision and Curriculum Development.

Wiliam, D. (2012). 'Feedback: Part of a System', Educational Leadership, 70(1) 31-34.

Chapter 5

It's all about the conversation

All change, even very large and powerful change, begins when a few people start talking with one another about something they care about. Simple conversations held at kitchen tables, or seated on the ground, or leaning against doorways are powerful means to start influencing and changing the world.

Margaret Wheatley (2002, p.9)

There is probably nothing that defines the human species more than conversation. We are irrepressibly social creatures and we thrive on communicating verbally and non-verbally with our families, friends and professional associates. In terms of our more recent evolution as a species, say the last 50,000 years, conversation has been the means in which we have shared craft knowledge in order to survive, identified our heroes and villains, developed the stories that have embedded our deeply held collective values and beliefs, and nurtured our collective intelligence. Brown and Isaacs (2005) write that

> since our earliest ancestors gathered in circles around the warmth of a fire, conversation has been our primary means for discovering what we care about, sharing knowledge, imagining the future and acting together to both survive and thrive... Conversation is our human way

of creating and sustaining or transforming – the realities in which we live. (p. XX)

Meaningful conversation is the intellectual and emotional crucible of learning and should be at the heart of every classroom and every school. However, we often associate conversation with casual chatting and fail to perceive its power for professional learning. If we want to move beyond the present failed system of teacher evaluation, we must pay deliberate attention to how we structure, craft and execute our conversations with colleagues. We have organized this chapter around five essential questions:

1. What is conversation?
2. What does truly meaningful conversation look and sound like?
3. How do meaningful conversations develop?
4. What are the norms of meaningful conversations?
5. What are some of the roles of the facilitator of meaningful conversations?

What is conversation?

The great Jewish philosopher Martin Buber (2004) posited that reality exists neither within me nor within you, but rather in the shared common domain that lies between 'I and Thou'. Given the propensity of our species to egocentricity, Buber's assertion is humbling. He suggests that we explore and negotiate the mysterious terrain of reality when we are in communion with others. Conversation is our primary means of such communion and is our most basic meaning-making tool. It is both the warp and weft of culture.

Human and animal culture can be defined in terms of social learning – how we learn from each other and in groups. Frans de Waal (2001), in *The Ape and the Sushi Master*, defines culture in terms of social learning and argues persuasively that animals, particularly primates, engage in social learning and cultural transmission. He cites numerous examples, including the now famous Japanese snow monkey's potato washing, as demonstrations of social learning.

However, more than any of the other creatures, we humans are social beings. According to the neuroscientist Matthew Lieberman (2013) we are hard wired to be social. As a species, humans are one of the most unlikely to survive when the individual is separated from a cooperative group. We have neither the speed of the gazelle, the strength of the leopard, nor the camouflage of the chameleon. What we do have is a monstrously large social brain that has allowed us to manage interpersonal and collective relationships so that we have become the most dominant species on earth.

Our need for social relationships is not only crucial to our physical survival but also to our emotional well being. The worst punishment that we can inflict on society's villains, short of execution, is solitary confinement because it is so counter to everything the social brain needs, wants and, in fact, demands.

Maslow was wrong

In 1943 Abraham Maslow published an article that included a genesis of his theory of human motivations – a hierarchy of human needs. He envisioned it as a pyramid with physiological needs at the base (food, water, shelter *etc*). The next level included elements of personal safety. Maslow labeled the third level 'Love and Belonging' and the final two levels 'Esteem' and 'Self-Actualization'.

The neuroscientist Matthew Lieberman (2013) is now suggesting, based on fMRI brain scans, that Maslow got it wrong. Food, water, shelter and personal security are not our most basic needs. Instead the base of Maslow's pyramid of human needs should be personal connectedness.

> Without social support infants will never survive to become adults who can provide for themselves… This restructuring of Maslow's pyramid tells us something critical about 'who we are'. Love and belonging might seem like a convenience we can live without, but our biology is built to thirst for connection because it is linked to our most basic survival needs. (p. 43)

The behavioral manifestation of our sense of belonging is the remarkable degree to which we work in collective groups. Cooperation is what makes human beings special and conversation is what fuels it.

Where did our massive brain come from?

Anthropologist and evolutionary psychologist Robin Dunbar (2010) is a leading proponent of the social brain hypothesis that suggests that there is a strong correlation between the massive human brain and our social needs. He has developed what has become known as Dunbar's number, the cognitive limit to the number of individuals with whom any one person can maintain stable relationships. These are relationships in which an individual knows who each person is and how each person relates to every other person (not a massive and shallow social network of Facebook friends).

He proposes that humans can only comfortably maintain 150 stable relationships. These are relationships of trust and intimacy, not just faces and names. Dunbar suggests that the enormous size of the human brain (the human brain is only 2% of our body mass but consumes 20% of our caloric intake) is a result of millions of years of managing social relationships – most recently our conversations.

Size does matter

In addition, fascinating work has also been undertaken in comparing encephalization quotients with social group size. Encephalization quotient (what anthropologists refer to as EQ) is the measure of relative brain size defined as the ratio between actual brain size and predicted brain size for an animal of a given size, which is hypothesized to be a rough estimate of the intelligence of the animal.

The EQ for rats and rabbits is about 0.4; cats weigh in at about 1, chimps at 2.5, bottlenose dolphins at 5, and humans at about 7.5. There appears to be a positive and linear progression between EQ and the social complexity of a species as demonstrated in maximum group size. The bigger the brain, the larger the social group.

The social brain hypothesis holds many implications for the optimal size of schools, leadership/teacher relationship ratios, and team size.

Conversations are the primary means by which humans manage complex social relationships. Dunbar proposes that language may have arisen as a 'cheap' means of social grooming, allowing early humans to maintain social cohesion efficiently. However, as we evolved as a species, our conversations became more and more complex.

It is through our conversations that interpersonal access is given and received, connections are made, unspoken contracts of reciprocity are forged, trust is developed, intimacy negotiated, data collected and analyzed, and meaning made.

Aunt Grace and the lawn mower paradox

As a child, Bill would often spend the Thanksgiving and Christmas holidays at the home of his Aunt Grace. After a huge celebration dinner, the table groaning with turkey, sweet potatoes, garden peas and overflowing gravy boats, the women of the family (the men withdrew to the living room to smoke and drink coffee) would gather in the kitchen to wash the dirty dishes. Just as the washing up commenced, Aunt Grace would dutifully announce: "Many hands make light work."

And she was absolutely correct. In terms of physical labor it is relatively easy to organize collaboration and reduce the workload on any one individual. One person scraped the plates, another washed and still others dried them.

Enter the dragon: the lawn mower paradox. Harvard cognitive scientist David Perkins (2003) suggests that it is vastly easier for six men to mow a lawn together than it is for six men to design a better lawn mower. Physical and cognitive collaboration are two very different creatures. Cognitive collaboration is complex and challenging and its effectiveness relies heavily on the quality of our conversations.

A high quality, meaningful conversation can be defined as a temporary and ephemeral union of minds through the deliberate use of language in which the co-construction and co-creation of meaning results in mental and emotional transformations that transcend time and place. Klimek, Ritzenhein, and Sullivan (2008) write:

> Authentic conversations are essential to social cohesion. They deepen, amplify, speed up, and strengthen the bonds of trust that are vital to group communication, cooperation, and survival. Through authentic conversation, groups propagate the traditions across generations, exchange the stories that confirm their identity, and bring forward the group's collective knowledge and wisdom. (p.69)

So what does high quality, meaningful conversation actually look and sound like?

Meaningful conversation may not be the norm in many schools or organizations for several reasons. First, in schools we often suffer from Organizational Attention Deficit Disorder (OADHD) (Goleman, 2013) in which the seemingly *urgent* crowds out the *important*. We come to believe that we have so much to do, most of it due yesterday, that we live in a frenetic world where internally focused and controlled attention is increasingly difficult.

Secondly, we believe in the primacy of accomplishment over learning. If we haven't accomplished a task and crossed it off a list, we haven't done our job. Adult learning tends to be gradual, invisible and hard to display as a demonstrable achievement – it therefore often gets placed on the back burner. There is that unspoken assumption that we are paid for teaching, not for learning.

And thirdly, we have, for the most part, little training in how to conduct deep, transformative conversations. When we are unsure of how to go about something, we often avoid it. Debilitating stress is often not so much about having too much to do, but rather being faced with challenges we do not know how to address.

Learning how to learn

Bill's first experience with a transformative conversation was in his senior year as an undergraduate. He was a literature major and had discovered a minor, but fascinating (at least to him) British author by the name of Charles Williams. A member of the Inkling Group of writers that included J R Tolkien and C S Lewis, Williams was a mystical Christian novelist, Arthurian scholar and a learned theologian. Among his other works, *The Descent of the Dove* is a history of the Holy Ghost in the Church. His intriguing novels present no demarcation between the natural and the supernatural worlds.

Bill wrote to the chairman of the English department at the university and requested that he be allowed to do an independent study on the novels of Charles Williams. Bill's request must have caused some discussion in the faculty lounge because in the end the proposed independent study resulted in a group that met once a week for nine weeks. The group was composed of a history professor, the academic dean of the College, a professor of philosophy, two women who would go on to study theology at Yale Seminary, and Bill.

The novels were challenging and often very esoteric, but the conversation was scintillating. Bill recognized that he was in the presence of masterful learners who used the art of conversation to create an understanding that would have been illusive to anyone of them on their own. In this communion there was profound intellectual humility. Confusion was nurtured and ignorance perceived as opportunity.

We were engaged in genuine collaborative inquiry. There were no experts. Charles Williams' novels were new to all of us. There was no competition or apparent need for ego-gratification. Questions, however clumsily framed, were treated with respect. There was psychological safety that permitted everyone the energy of cognitive and at times emotional discomfort.

Bill listened, sometimes in awe, at the deliberate and careful use of language, the struggle for accuracy and precision on the part of his professors and the intimacy of how participants made personal connections between the fiction and their own personal lives.

It was as though we were building something in the middle of the room. Everyone contributed and was part of the process. There was not only union, but communion. We weren't building a concrete structure, but we might have been. It was just as real – a collective understanding and appreciation of the mysteries of human nature. There was honesty, intellectual rigor, compassion, deep insight that resulted in evolving understanding – all on display in that collective domain between 'I and Thou'.

In the final gathering of the Williams study group, participants were asked to describe the experience that we had undergone. The words and phrases that emerged included: enlightening, transformative, transcendental, and spiritually nourishing.

Transformative conversation includes many dimensions. First and foremost, meaningful conversation is an exercise in *listening*. It is an inquiry into the ideas and assumptions that requires inferential and interpretive listening. It is a communal search for deeper meaning and as such it must be sensitive to different people's tolerance for uncertainty and ambiguity. It brings into the light of day assumptions that had hitherto been unexamined; it alters the tacit infrastructure of thought.

Secondly it tends to be other-focused. In other words, participants enter with deliberately restrained autobiographies. While most of us can never truly leave ourselves behind, we need the discipline to quarantine our egos for the duration of the conversation, to separate issues and identity so that ideas become the collective 'property' of the group. Deep conversations involve deliberate mindfulness and 'Me' is often the inhibitor of mindfulness. Goleman (2013) writes 'It's not the chatter of people around us that is the most powerful distractor, but rather the chatter of our own minds.' (p. 48)

In a wonderfully evocative book, *The Art and Science of Portraiture*, Lawrence-Lightfoot and Davis (1997) describe in detail the subtle and complex relationship between the ethnographic portraiturist (the researcher) and her subjects. The meaningful conversation contains many of the elements of this detached and yet decidedly humane and intimate relationship. We will explore more similarities between ethnographic research and meaningful conversation when we come to look at the role of the conversation facilitator.

What enhances collective intelligence?

Meaningful conversations enhance the collective intelligence of the group (Powell & Kusuma-Powell, 2013). Research from MIT (Woolley, *et. al*, 2010) makes it abundantly clear that collective intelligence is real and is measurable and it is demonstrated in conversation. Woolley and her research colleagues tested a large group of subjects for individual intelligence (IQ) and then put them into random groups that were assigned complex problems to solve.

As the results were analyzed, the researchers attempted to identify variables that had contributed to enhanced collective intelligence. They found no correlation between the average individual intelligence and the performance of groups. In other words, smart individuals did not necessarily make smart groups – something that is borne out in politics on a daily basis. History is replete with very bright individuals who came together to make stupid decisions.

However, the MIT researchers did find three variables that were positively correlated to enhanced collective intelligence and they all have to do with the art of meaningful conversation.

The first was turn-taking, the more or less equitable contribution of all group members to the conversation. The researchers found that when there was a single dominant member of the group, collective intelligence suffered accordingly. Turn-taking is a form of social fairness, sharing as equitably as possible the contributions to the conversation. Lieberman (2013) suggests that fairness is one of the signs that we are socially connected, that others value us and when resources are in short supply (including meeting time) we are likely to receive an equitable portion.

Many of us have thought of fairness as a 'hygiene factor', an aspect of life that has the power to dissatisfy (in its absence), but has no power to cause us a sense of satisfaction. In other words, we are annoyed and indignant when we perceive that we have been treated unfairly. If we are cut off or dismissed in a conversation, many times we will withdraw from it. We sometimes think of fairness like oxygen: we only notice it when it is in short supply. However, Lieberman (2013) takes issue with this idea and writes that the same brain regions that are associated with physical pleasure, such as eating chocolate, respond to being treated fairly. 'In a sense, then, fairness is like chocolate' (p. 75). Turn-taking is a form of social fairness and without it conversations cannot be truly meaningful.

The second variable identified by the MIT researchers was social sensitivity. Individuals in the research design were tested for social sensitivity by way of Simon Baron-Cohen's (2001) *Reading the Mind in the Eyes Test - Revised*, in which photographs are shown to the subject with all facial expression masked except the eyes. The subject is then asked to identify the emotion that the photograph is displaying. The MIT researchers found a positive correlation between the presence of individuals who scored high on this test of non-verbal social sensitivity in groups that exhibited high collective intelligence.

Social sensitivity requires a special kind of focus attention – a social mindfulness. Some people seem to be born with masses of this emotional intelligence. Others, less so. However, we now know that social sensitivity can be developed and emotional intelligence can be learned. It is all a matter of what we select to pay attention to.

Attention actually determines what we will see and hear. The brain will admit external stimuli on the basis of a number of filters of perception, among them: culture, gender, developmental level, cognitive style, or belief systems. Often when we don't have the metaphor, we can't see the object. Social sensitivity is paying close and deliberate attention to self and others.

When we do so, we gain influence over how we construct these perceptions and we have an opportunity to modify them. Steven Wollf (as cited in Goleman, 2013), a principal at GEI Partners, writes:

> To harvest the collective wisdom of the group you need two things: mindful presence and a sense of safety. You need a shared mental model that this is a safe place... Being present means being aware of what's going on and inquiring into it. I've learned to appreciate negative emotions – it's not that I enjoy them, but that they signal a pot of gold at the end of the rainbow if we can stay present to them. (p. 244)

It is often useful to recall Daniel Goleman's assertion: 'A wealth of information creates a poverty of attention.' (2013, p. 9)

The third factor that the MIT researchers identified as a characteristic of high intelligence groups was the presence of women. This was not a diversity factor, but rather a linear progression. Statistically, the more women in a group, the smarter the group. The researchers speculated that this finding may be related to social sensitivity since, in general, women tend to score higher on test of social sensitivity than men do.

Social sensitivity has at its foundation empathetic regard; the capacity we have for entering the perspective of another person, appreciating it and respecting it – particularly when we may not be in agreement with it. The psychologist Rollo May (in Lawrence-Lightfoot & Davis, 1997) writes that empathy is

> learning to relax mentally and spiritually as well as physically, learning to let one's self go into the other person with a willingness to be changed in the process, (p.97 cited in Portraiture p. 147)

May perceives that empathy is the opposite of egocentricity.

> In this identification real understanding between people can take place; without it, in fact, no understanding is possible. (In Lawrence Lightfoot & Davis, 1997 p.147)

There is a well-known relationship between empathetic regard and power disparity. The powerful (*ie* those from an affluent, dominant culture) tend to exhibit less empathy than cultural minorities and the disenfranchised. Martin Luther King Jr commented on this many times in his reflections on race relations in the United States. In meaningful conversation, power disparity needs to be mitigated as much as possible. We enter the conversation as co-equals, leaving rank and authority at the door. Ascribed power by dint of position is best used very sparingly and has no positive function in collaborative inquiry.

Social sensitivity can produce relational trust, which Bryk and Schneider (2004) define as recognizing our dependency on others. Dependency on others in turn produces vulnerability and this can result in a sense of anxiety. Trust is our capacity to reduce the anxiety while at the same time embrace the vulnerability. It is crucial in transformative conversations.

Another feature of meaningful conversations is intimacy negotiation. Generally, professional conversations are about information that will be shared or responded to voluntarily. We are not counselors or therapists – we are conversationalists. Therefore we do not go into the realm of the intimate, except by specific invitation.

Order is a necessary condition for human understanding. However, order is not the same as rigidity and formulaic rules and regulations. If you want to kill creative and critical thought in conversations use Roberts' Rules of Order. Nevertheless we do need structure. In figure 1, we have constructed a Developmental Continuum for Meaningful Conversations that contains descriptions of structure, interpersonal interaction, content boundaries, and facilitation from the level of Casual Meetings to Transformative Conversations.

The careful reader will notice an interesting development. Levels one and two (Casually Organized and Extrinsically Organized) are the domain of meetings. Meaningful Conversations begins to emerge at level three (Intrinsically Organized). Also note that formal structure predominates at level two and to some degree at level three and actually diminishes in level four. Creative and critical thought is self-directed, often spontaneous and therefore may appear messy.

How do conversations develop in respect to meaningfulness?
Developmental Continuum for Meaningful Conversations

Component of Conversation/ Levels of Development	Structure of Conversation	Interpersonal interaction	Content Boundaries	Facilitation
Level 1: Casual Organization	While a written agenda may not be circulated in advance of the meeting, participants have an idea of what is going to be discussed and what the overall outcome is likely to be. The conversation is fluid and drifts between dialogue and discussion, which may encourage spontaneity but also frustrate some participants. Meetings may meander and take considerable time. Often there is concern for democratic practices – everyone's voice being heard and reaching consensus. The meeting may come to closure or it may run out of time.	The group is exploring its team dynamics and identity. It is conscious of the need to pay attention to how they are working together. There may be a pleasant sense of camaraderie. Participants may enjoy sharing 'war stories'. Appropriate humor may be present. However the group may be conflict adverse in that it associates disagreements with destructive personal conflict. Loyalty may masquerade as trust and conviviality as respect. When the group does accomplish something, it celebrates with considerable relish.	Loose and fluid. The focus of the meeting may begin in one place but move on to tangents. This style may suit those who have a proclivity toward the abstract random, but may be frustrating to the concrete sequential engineers. In casual meetings there may be present the illusion of accomplishment – the notion that because we have talked about something we have addressed it effectively.	There may be an ascribed facilitator or meeting chairperson or this may be a rotating responsibility. The primary goal of the facilitator is to keep the conversation going. The facilitator may attempt to get reticent participants to contribute, but may be perplexed at how to constrain more dominant group members. The facilitator is keen to explore group reflective protocols.

Component of Conversation/ Levels of Development	Structure of Conversation	Interpersonal interaction	Content Boundaries	Facilitation
Level 2: Extrinsic Organization	The group has an agenda in advance of the meeting and has a clear idea of the topics under consideration. The group understands the difference between dialogue and discussion and explicitly determines which will be most effective given the topics and content being dealt with. The group is beginning to become familiar with certain meeting protocols. Time limits may be set for certain items and the minutes will reflect action items and who is responsible for implementation. Participants are respectful of each other's time and come to the meeting prepared. The outcome of the meeting is efficiency and closure on a topic or issue.	The norms of collaboration have been clearly understood and the participants are keen to practice their new skills. Genuine listening is present some of the time and is demonstrated in pausing, paraphrasing and posing questions. There are still some moments of unproductive listening – particularly autobiographical listening. Because these skills are still developing, they may be applied intermittently – when the participant remembers them. There are moments of meaningful conversations. The boundaries of intimacy may be unclear and this may make some participants uncomfortable. Respect is present and trust is developing.	There is a fixed agenda and a strong emphasis on staying focused on the issue at hand. The meeting is perceived to be successful when focus is maintained on one piece of content and the group manages to reach closure on it. On occasion, the single-minded focus on one central piece of content can blind a group to other external connections that may be fruitful.	There is strong facilitation. The facilitator sets an explicit structure for the conversation, reminding participants about the norms of the conversation. Conversational efficiency is of primary importance. The facilitator perceives that it is his or her job to keep the group on task – focused on the issue at hand. Off-the-topic observations or comments are placed in 'the parking lot'. The facilitator may close the meeting by having the participants inventory their strengths and weaknesses on the norms of collaboration and engage them in goal setting for future meetings. The facilitator may be exploring the use of protocols.

Component of Conversation/ Levels of Development	Structure of Conversation	Interpersonal interaction	Content Boundaries	Facilitation
Level 3: Intrinsic Organization	The group has developed together and understands that inquiry is central to collective meaning making. Accordingly dialogue precedes discussion. The group may employ specific reflective and problem resolving protocols. Membership has internalized the structure of collaborative inquiry and, for the most part is self-policing in terms of staying focused. The outcome of the conversation may be new learning.	Group members have practiced and internalized the norms of collaboration and have developed inferential listening skills. They use those inferential listening skills to frame reflective questions designed to build intellectual and emotional capacity in other members of the group. There is strong group cohesion, but not at the expense of deep critical thought. Trust and respect are present. Cognitive conflict is sought after.	The group comes together around a topic or concept that has cross- disciplinary implications. While multiple perspectives are invited and welcomed, there is still the notion of discrete areas of expertise and some discomfort with boundary crossing.	The facilitation is subtle because, through deliberate practice the group has internalized the norms of collaboration. The conversation is thoughtful with frequent pauses. Silence is respected. There may be an ascribed facilitator, but increasingly members of the group function effectively without external intervention. They are learning to facilitate both themselves and others.

Component of Conversation/ Levels of Development	Structure of Conversation	Interpersonal interaction	Content Boundaries	Facilitation
Level 4: Transformative Organization	The structure of the conversation may appear loose and fluid to an outside observer because of its spontaneity and creativity. Someone unfamiliar with transformational conversation might perceive it as unstructured and messy. However, the participants have internalized the external structure. There is little need for an imposed structure. The outcome of the conversation is transformative learning, cognitive shift, sudden new connections or ideas that may modify existing beliefs and values.	Participants bring themselves to the conversation, but not their egos. They come with values, beliefs, knowledge, and attitudes, but without the need to control. Trust is high. Participants are socially sensitive. They engage in deep exchanges, listening intently to each other, seeking clarification and probing for greater specificity. Intimacy negotiation is by invitation. Participants may enter a state of 'flow'. The conversation becomes effortless and energy producing as opposed to energy consuming. Some may actually lose themselves in the conversation and become unaware of the passage of time. New insights and gestalts are shared.	The group comes together around complex, trans-disciplinary questions that have no immediate answer or solution. The right-to-boundary-trespass is implicitly understood as a healthy norm of collaborative inquiry. The group has mapped mental right-of-ways. The rich connections from disparate disciplines stimulate creativity and forge new insights and connections.	Facilitation is organic – shared and distributed between and among group members. It is every one's responsibility to stay focused, listen with empathy and understanding, and construct questions that will engage the collective group in deeper and more meaningful thought.

Figure 1

The way we talk mirrors the way we think

Our conversations often reflect the frameworks within which we think. For example, if we hear excessive externalizing of blame, we may be dealing with someone with low internal efficacy. In Cognitive Coaching (Costa & Garmston, 2002) training, participants are sensitized to listen inferentially for low and high resourcefulness in five states of mind: efficacy; consciousness; flexibility; craftsmanship; and interdependence and to craft mediative questions that will support the person being coached to become more resourceful in a particular state of mind.

The constraints that we place on our oral language may reflect the limits that we place on our cognitive processes. Each of us develops a multitude of unconscious habits of mind and these patterns are reflected in our conversations. Smalley & Winston (2010) call the investigation of these thought patterns the first step in practicing mindfulness, in becoming fully present.

Kegan and Lahey (2001) suggest that in transforming the way in which we talk, we can actually influence the way in which we work. They describe seven transformations; each begins with a shift from a habitual, unexamined and non-reflective pattern to a more deliberate and more reflective stance. The transformations are:

> From the language of complaint to the language of commitment.
>
> From the language of blame to the language of personal responsibility.
>
> From the language of New Year's Resolutions to the language of competing commitments.
>
> From the language of big assumptions that hold us to the language of assumptions that we hold.
>
> From the language of prizes and praising to the language of ongoing regard.
>
> From the language of rules and policies to the language of public agreements.
>
> From the language of constructive criticism to the language of deconstructive criticism. (2001)

What are some norms of meaningful conversations?

Meaningful conversations are characterized by participants striving for accuracy and precision in language. They recognize that there is a powerful connection between the thoughtfulness of language and precision of thought. We may hear 'oral editing' when a participant pauses to reframe a thought or select a more appropriate or insightful phrase. And as the conversation grows rich with abstractions, we will hear others inquiring into how specifically certain words and phrases are being used. The group seeks after common definitions and often finds itself paying special attention to a thorny preposition or a less than specific adjective. And from this emerges a balanced, mutual and generous probing-perspective.

Transformative conversations require both mindfulness and emotional self-regulation. We recognize that others have cognitive styles that may clash with our own. Ochan has a very different style to that of Bill. She likes to explore the topography, venture off the beaten path and slowly she will come to map the terrain. Bill on the other hand is concrete, sequential and wants a clear, linear, step-by-step blueprint to follow. With mindfulness, emotional regulation and a little luck, both Ochan and Bill will get to the end of this book.

Emotional regulation does not imply sterile scientific objectivity. On the contrary, the participant in meaningful conversation is a highly engaged, compassionate researcher. Ethnographer Michael Jackson writes:

> To compare notes on experience with someone else presumes and creates a common ground, and the understanding arrived at takes its validity not from our detachment and objectivity but from the very possibility of our mutuality, the existence of the relationship itself. (Jackson, in Lawrence-Lightfoot & Davis, 1977, p. 136)

There is an organic quality to rich conversation that evokes Wordsworth's definition of poetry: 'emotions recollected in tranquility.'

Meaningful conversations are constant negotiation and renegotiation of relationships. Reflecting on the issue of relationships in professional research, Lawrence-Lightfoot (1997) writes:

> We see relationships as more than vehicles for data gathering, more than points of access. We see them as central to the empirical, ethical, and humanistic dimensions of research design, as evolving and changing processes of human encounter. (p. 138)

Deep conversation takes learning from the episodic – in which it applies to only one situation anchored in one moment in time, and makes it generalizable. This means that we can take the new insight and apply it in new and novel situations in the future. The new connections are transferable – hopefully to the classroom.

Truly meaningful conversations may follow a process that we refer to as 'the data to wisdom' continuum (Powell & Kusuma-Powell, 2013). Transformational learning can involve a progression through the following stages:

Anticipation.

Data collection.

Information formation.

Knowledge development.

Wisdom emergence.

Anticipation

When faced with a complex issue or topic, groups may be well served by spending a little time anticipating the inquiry process. Wellman & Lipton (2004) refer to this stage as 'Activating and Engaging' and suggest that the following questions may prime the inquiry pump: what are some predictions we are making? With what assumptions are we inquiring? What are some possibilities for learning?

Data collection

Data represents the raw material of inquiry. It is usually observable, factually accurate, neutral and meaningless without interpretation. For example, the fact that staff absenteeism has risen by 30% is data. At this point, we have no idea why.

Information formation

When we start to arrange data, we see the beginning of pattern making. We observe and analyze; we look for commonalities and outliers. We need at this point to be careful that we don't reach premature conclusions. Lipton and Wellman (2004) call this stage 'Exploring and Discovering'. We may ask ourselves what seems surprising or unexpected. What may be some things that we have not yet explored? For example, we recognize that the rise in staff absenteeism is primarily in the secondary school, which has also been the venue of a series of labor grievances. However, we may wish to avoid the possibly premature and erroneous conclusion that the absenteeism is associated with the grievances.

Knowledge development

In order to move information to knowledge we need to engage in the rigorous process of critical thinking: deep analysis; comparison; synthesis; and evaluation. We need to make inferences, put forth explanations and tentative conclusions by way of questions. We need to generate theories and test them against external reality. At this point we may also discover that our data set is incomplete.

This is hard cognitive labor that benefits enormously from collaborative effort. Lipton and Wellman (2004) refer to this stage as 'Organizing and Integrating'. In our example of staff absenteeism, we might discover additional patterns within patterns. Perhaps the absences affect one gender, racial or ethnic group more than another. We might frame a question accordingly and attempt to test it against reality.

Wisdom emergence

Knowledge is not the same as wisdom. Wisdom goes beyond the available meaning in order to arrive at new insights and perspectives, based upon our learning and experience. Wisdom is where transformational learning takes place. It often involves a sudden cognitive shift, a new connection, an alternative perception or a profound gestalt. In our example, the knowledge that a particular cultural or ethnic group of teachers may be feeling disenfranchised can come to be perceived as an opportunity for greater mutual understanding.

	Guidelines for meaningful conversation
1.	**Content:** Start with a single question that is simply worded but rich in complex interpretation. Brown and Issacs (2005) conducted a World Café Conversation for the Singapore Police Department that lasted three hours around the single question: In what ways do the Singapore Police show that they care?
2.	**Pacing:** Thoughtful conversations are punctuated with pauses. These short periods of silence send the message that in this conversation thinking is not only permissible, but also expected. Pausing also prevents personalized conflict and makes it more likely that reticent participants will contribute. 'Silences speak about points of confusion or resistance, or they indicate ambivalence or evasion, or they hide private feelings or make a dramatic point.' (Lawrence-Lightfoot, 1997, P. 100). Silence heralds opportunity and is much too important to ignore.
3.	**Balancing skepticism and appreciation:** Adults grow cognitively, emotionally and spiritually when they are in healthy holding environments; in other words when they are presented with developmentally appropriate supports and challenges (Drago-Severson, 2009). Groups that deliberately balance rigorous scrutiny with explicit interpersonal support often achieve transformational learning. Begin with inquiry; explore ideas and possibilities that enhance collective understanding. All too often, meaningful conversation is subverted when one member of the group voices an opinion too quickly and then feels the need to defend it or score points. Such advocacy can serve to shut down the contributions of other group members.
4.	**Structure:** Meaningful conversations are more likely to occur when the structure, boundaries, and commitments of the relationship are made explicit from the start. We spend time talking about how we will talk with each other. We generate essential understandings about the nature of conversation, how we will manage conflict. We make explicit simple housekeeping rules (*eg* no interruptions).
5.	**Unity:** We encourage participants to use the second person pronoun 'we' as opposed to the first person pronoun 'I'. The use of 'we' supports group cohesion, especially when we talk about 'our school' or 'our students' as opposed to 'my school' or 'my students'.
6.	**Timing:** Probably the most common barrier to meaningful conversations is the perception that there isn't time for them. If we only learn from reflection on experience (not from experience itself), then there can be no more important activity for a teacher to engage in than reflective inquiry. We need to deliberately carve out sacred time for it. However, meaningful conversations demand intense controlled attention and probably should be limited at the start at least to no more than 20-30 minutes.
7.	**Conversational repair:** On occasion, conversation may become de-railed. Misunderstanding can emerge that can lead to imprecise attribution of intention. This can lead to a lack of psychological safety, feelings of anxiety and intimidation, anger and frustration or withdrawal. 'I have no value in this group. I'm never listened to. I might as well not be here at all.' Neuroscientist Matthew Lieberman (2013) has identified that the same pain centers in the brain are activated when one feels physical pain and one feels social pain (humiliation, intimidation, fear, shame, *etc.*) 'Social pain is real pain just as physical pain is real pain. Understanding this has important consequences for how we think about the social distress that we and those around us experience' (p. 46). Social sensitivity and mindfulness alert us to the social distress in others and makes us aware of opportunities to intervene in order to honor, affirm and repair.

Figure 2.

What are some of the roles of a facilitator of meaningful conversation?

Unless there is a very well-established and mature collaborative group, a skilled facilitator is a necessity. The stance of the conversation facilitator is one of acceptance, generosity, discernment and challenge, always encouraging the participants to express their strengths, values, beliefs, passions and insights. Deep reflection demands a great deal of controlled attention. 'The more distracted we are, the more shallow our reflections, likewise the shorter our reflections and the more trivial they are likely to be' (Goleman, 2013 p. 19).

One highly skilled facilitator that we have worked with began every meeting with a 'distraction parking lot' – a space on a large white board for participants to write what issues were likely to distract then from focus on the conversation. The distractors were not forgotten but were 'parked' for the duration of the conversation.

First and foremost, the skilled facilitator is an active and authentic listener – a mirror to reflect emotion and content. The speaker should be able to see 'refracted resonance' in the facilitator's eyes (Lawrence-Lightfoot & Davis, 1997, p. 149). The facilitator listens for patterns, for 'marker words' (words that may be associated with strong emotions), repetitive refrains, and figurative language (metaphorical styles). The facilitator brings interpretive insight and analytic scrutiny to the collection of data.

Skillful facilitation is a demonstration of deliberate social mindfulness. The facilitator achieves this through paraphrasing participants and posing challenging, but psychologically safe questions; questions that are designed to be other-centered. In Cognitive Coaching, we stress the mediative pattern of pausing, paraphrasing, pausing, and posing questions. The facilitator strives for a form of meta-awareness and listens between the lines and beneath the surface of the words, identifying phrases, facial expressions and tones of voice that indicate the presence of treasures that the group may have buried in 'graves of indifference or suppression' (Goleman, 2103, p. 75).

The facilitator is sensitive to both verbal and nonverbal communication and is alert to the behavioral manifestations of deep thinking. The outward displays of reflection include changes to facial expression, complexion, shift of eyes (either looking up or downward), perhaps a momentary dazed expression or a prolonged pause. These are some of the indicators that deep thinking is going on and the facilitator should ensure that the process is not interrupted.

The conversation facilitator also strives to equalize status amongst participants as power disparity will inhibit idea flow. Our work in Adaptive Schools (Garmston & Wellman, 2009) suggests that as a general rule the facilitator should not be an individual with either position authority (*eg* the principal) or knowledge authority (the expert). These roles are crucial to the dialogue and discussion about content. The facilitator, on the other hand, needs to be content-neutral and focused on the process and dynamics of the group.

The facilitator may also be the connector and the coherence-maker. He or she listens beneath the surface for the linkages in ideas and then makes those explicit. These connections are the glue that binds the conversation together. The facilitator gathers, organizes, and scrutinizes the convergent threads of the conversation – weaving coherence out of themes that the conversationalists might have experienced as unrelated or incoherent.

The facilitator engages in an iterative process of listening for patterns in the emerging data that will direct and shape future subsequent data collection. Coherence is the 'orderly, logical, and aesthetically consistent relation of the parts, when all the pieces fall into place and we can see the pattern clearly' (Lawrence-Lightfoot & Davis, 1997, p. 255). Coherence-making is especially important at times of conversational transition.

The facilitator is also the orchestrator of differing modes of reflection and inquiry. Different people need to edit their thoughts in different ways. Some do well in oral exchanges. Others need a brief time for written reflection. Still others will benefit from a visual representation. We remember a highly skilled facilitator assigning a group of teachers homework that included making a non-verbal (no words) collage that represented success for a struggling student that they were currently teaching. The following day each teacher made a brief presentation on the images and visual metaphors they had selected. A lively and insightful conversation ensued. Such orchestration needs to be part of facilitation.

The skilled facilitator needs to be a miner of insight. Carl Rogers defines insight as 'a process of becoming sufficiently free to look at old facts in new ways, an experience of discovering new relationships among familiar attitudes, a willingness to accept the implications of well-known material' (in Lawrence-Lightfoot & Davis, 1997, p. 147).

The facilitator poses questions that take the conversation beneath superficiality. The facilitator listens beneath the surface of the conversation for three inquiry blind alleys that may interrupt or close down fruitful lines of exploration. These are:

Premature closure: This can be the superficial generalization that shuts down thought. For example, we may hear this in a child study team meeting when a participant concludes: 'the child is exhibiting attention seeking behavior'. The label may give the false impression of a new insight, but may actually represent facile thinking or simplistic logic. The label actually may interrupt fruitful lines of inquiry and actually bring the conversation to premature closure.

Seduction by status: A very common *conversatio interruptus*, this involves the overweighting of comments of an esteemed authority or an articulate, well-informed participant. For example when a colleague known for his erudition begins "Professor Howard Gardner from Harvard says that..."

Excessive group cohesion: This is when the facilitator is co-opted into the groupthink of the participants and loses perspective and detachment.

The facilitator leaves his/her pre-determined outcomes at the door and embraces the accident, hazard and chance of authentic human interaction. The facilitator is not action oriented. The conversation doesn't need to end with 'action points' or 'a way forward'. This suspension of 'doing' is difficult for some task-oriented individuals who have a proclivity to think like engineers. They see a problem or task and they see only the possible solutions or the jobs to be undertaken; they can be unconscious of the people and the process surrounding them. The purpose of the conversation is the *conversation* and the rich new insight and connections that may emerge from it. The utility is in the thinking – not in solving or doing.

The facilitator is the nurturer of the gestalt. The process is 'both systematic and creative, structured and organic, disciplined and intuitive' (Lawrence-Lightfoot & Davis, 1997 p.244). We are reminded of the Persian Fairy story of the Princes of Serendip who were always making chance discoveries of things that they were not in search of. The skilled facilitator listens at the fringes of the conversation for just such accidental but beneficent opportunities.

The facilitator is also the interpreter of the intentionality of others. He or she presumes positive intentions on behalf of the participants. We have, according to Lieberman, an inescapable inclination to see and understand others in terms of their internal mental processes (Lieberman, 2013 p. 106). We are drawn inextricably towards understanding the intentionality of others. When we experience confusion about another person's intentionality we will quickly fill the void – many times with less than generous attributions. Our obsession with the motivation of others probably has its roots in our evolution and in our hyper-sensitive threat detection mechanisms.

However, facilitators of deep conversations need to be in conscious charge of their positive presuppositions. When facilitators hear, see or intuit the deviant voice, they must move towards the danger and strive to uncover the positive intentionality. The facilitator is not a Pollyanna basking in excessive optimism or naiveté, but rather a hard-nosed, gentle realist, knowing that every human behavior is for a reason. And, as our colleague and friend Bob Garmston is fond of saying:

> However inappropriate a behavior may seem on first impression, for the most part people make the best decisions they can with the information and perceptions that are currently available to them.

The facilitator sets aside the old unproductive habits of exerting control, seeking comfort, driving task achievement, and coming to closure. At times the facilitator must even set aside the need for comprehension in order to submit to the rich complexity and instability of authentic human interaction. When the facilitators are able to suspend their own involvement to observe what's going on, to take the balcony view, they are provided with a mindful awareness of the interaction without being completely reactive.

The facilitator needs also to be the identifier of the 'deviant voice' – the voice that contrasts with the norm of the conversational flow. The deviant voice represents a divergence in perspective and when handled skillfully can add richness and deeper perception to the conversation. This

> idiosyncratic stance helps us see the quality and contours of the convergent themes more clearly. The deviant voice is also useful in encouraging the skeptical, counterintuitive stance... (Lawrence-Lightfoot & Davis, 1997, p.193)

Ultimately the facilitator needs to be a seeker after the 'good'. He or she needs to find and deconstruct the exemplary whether that is in the area of instructional effectiveness, content knowledge, interpersonal skills or professional reflection. When we explicitly look for strength, resilience and creativity, this 'generous stance opens up a space for the expression of the weakness, imperfection, and vulnerability that inevitably compromise the goodness' (Lawrence-Lightfoot, 1997, p. 158).

In closing

Conversation is a critical element in social learning and in developing self-directed teacher learners. It is often taken for granted, yielding superficial exchanges that waste precious time – although such conversations often masquerade as 'meetings'. Meaningful conversations are deliberate, thoughtful, mutual, reflective and take considerable practice and skill.

References

Baron-Cohen S., Wheelwright S., Hill J., Raste Y., Plumb I. (2001). The 'reading the mind in the eyes' test revised version: a study with normal adults, and adults with Asperger syndrome or high-functioning autism. J. Child Psychol. Psychiatry 42, 241–25110.1017/S0021963001266979.

Brown, J. & Isaacs,D. (2005). The World Café: Shaping our futures through conversations that matter. San Francisco: Berret-Koehler Publishers.

Bryk, A., & Schneider,B. (2004). Trust in schools: A core resource for improvement. New York: The Russell Sage Foundation.

Buber, M. (2004). I and Thou. London: Continuum International Publishing Group.

De Waal, F. (2001). The ape and the sushi master: Reflections of a primatologist. New York: Basic Books.

Drago-Seversen, E. (2009). Leading adult learning: Supporting adult learning in our schools. Thousand Oaks, CA: Corwin Press.

Dunbar, R. (2010). How many friends does one person need?: Dunbar's number and other evolutionary quirks. London: Faber & Faber.

Garmston, R. & Wellman, B. (2009) The adaptive school: A Sourcebook for Developing Collaborative Groups, Norwood, MA.: Christopher-Gordon Publishers.

Goleman, D. (2013). Focus: The hidden driver of Excellence, New York, NY. HarperCollins.

Kegan, R. & Lahey, L.L. (2001). How the way we talk can change the way we work: Seven language transformations. San Francisco: Jossey-Bass.

Klimek, K.L., Ritzenhein, E. & Sullivan, (2008). Generative leadership: Shaping new futures for today's schools. Thousand Oaks, CA: Corwin Press.

Lawrence-Lightfoot, S. & Davis, J. (1997). The art and science of portraiture. San Francisco: Jossey-Bas.

Lieberman, M. (2013). Social: Why our brain are wired to connect. New York: Crown Publishers.

Maslow, A. (1943). 'A theory of human motivation', Psychological Review 50(4) 370-96.

May, R. (1953). Man's search for himself. New York: Delta Books.

Perkins, D., (2003). King Arthur's round table: How collaborative conversations create smart organizations. Hoboken, NJ: John Wiley & Sons.

Powell, W. & Kusuma-Powell, O. (2013). The OIQ Factor: Raising the organizational intelligence of your school. Woodbridge, UK: John Catt Educational.

Smalley, S.L. & Winston, D., (2010). Fully present: The science, art and practice of Mindfulness. Philadelphia, PA: DaCapo Press.

Wellman, B. & Lipton, L. (2004), Data Driven Dialogue: A facilitator's guide to collaborative inquiry. Arlington, MA: MiraVia LLC.

Wheatley, M. (2002). Turning to one another: Simple conversations to restore hope to the future. San Francisco: Berrett-Koehler.

Woolley, A., Chabris, C., Pentland, A., Hashmi, N., & Malone, T. (2010) 'Evidence for a collective intelligence factor in the performance of human groups', Science, 330(6004) 686-688.

Chapter 6

It's all about coherence

One of the themes in E M Forster's (2002) *Howards End*, first published in 1910, is the critical importance of making connections. The author exhorts us to 'only connect!' It is the making of connections that allow Forster's characters to move from arrogance to humility and from destructive chaos to a greater sense of benevolent unity. Connections are no less important in our schools because they are the web of emerging coherence.

Whole to part learning

Most of us learn better and more effectively when we work from whole to part. What this means is that we need the big picture first and then we fit the details into to it (Brooks & Brooks, 1999). Imagine receiving a birthday present, a kit containing 75 unassembled pieces that when put together will form your new set of kitchen cabinets. The first thing most of us will do is look for the illustration of what the assembled product looks like. We need the big picture before dealing with the nuts and screws.

This is a principle that is often forgotten or ignored in schools. In the fragmented structure of schools (with our division into grades, specialists, subjects, departments *etc*), we find it difficult to see beyond the shadows of our own, narrow pigeonhole. This is one reason that curriculum articulation and mapping have proved so illusive even in the best of schools. Many schools lack coherence and, as a result, student and teacher learning suffer.

The geometry of personal meaning

In the eighth grade Bill was introduced to geometry. The teacher immediately launched into the content of the course. Bill writes that 'we began by looking at the perimeter of two-dimensional objects; we then moved on to area, and then to volume.' Bill struggled to memorize the required formulas and by November was just barely passing the course.

At the end of that month, there was a large and important test upon which Bill's semester grade hinged. He attempted to study for the test but became increasingly frustrated in his efforts. Finally, he sought help from Malcolm, an older student who was known to be good at mathematics. Malcolm started out by asking Bill what he didn't understand. Like many confused and anxious students, Bill didn't know what he didn't understand. Then Malcolm did something unusual. Instead of plunging into the nitty gritty of geometry, he simply asked Bill what geometry was all about. Malcolm seemed to intuitively understand that Bill was missing the big picture. Bill's mind was so crowded with fragments of unconnected information; with half memorized formulas and algorithms that nothing seemed to make sense and the resulting stress further inhibited understanding.

Malcolm spent no more than an hour with Bill, supporting him in understanding the big picture, the interconnectedness of geometry. Malcolm was a natural teacher and he enabled Bill to construct personal meaning. Bill did extremely well on the big test and had 'As' in geometry for the rest of the year. Such is the power of coherence making.

Adults, no less than children, need coherence in their learning. Humans are pattern-seeking creatures. Even from a very early age we look for and identify patterns. These can be as simple as the activities that form our daily routine. We attend school during the daylight hours on weekdays. At 10 o'clock we have recess and lunch is at noon. The bus that takes us home leaves at 3.30pm. As we grow older the patterns become subtler and more complex. They can include the verbal and non-verbal behavior that indicates the emotions and moods of our parents, siblings and friends or being able to read the teacher's expectations so that we can play that school game with success.

Pattern-making is all about identifying systematic or logical connections. It is about glimpses of thematic or cognitive consistency, the integration of diverse elements, relationships or values into a meaningful whole.

A return visit to the Island School

Let's make a return visit to the Island School that we met in chapter five. As you will recall the Island School had innovation on the front burner. It had a team of learning coaches whose responsibility it was to stay up to date on recent research and developments in education and psychology and bring those initiatives to the teachers at the school. New books on teaching and learning arrived at the school weekly. Articles were posted on the school's electronic bulletin board. Teachers were regularly invited to participate in webinars. The administration and faculty were extremely proud of being a 'cutting edge school' and saw themselves as a center of teacher learning in their region.

And there was no question that an enormous amount of teacher learning was taking place. However, like Bill's initial experience with geometry, the learning was fragmented and unconnected – an uncoordinated banquet that left the diners with serious cognitive indigestion. At the time of our visit, the previous six months had seen the visits of seven external consultants who had made presentations on an array of important but seemingly unrelated topics, in addition to myriad internally-led teacher workshops.

One of the primary functions of the brain is to make connections and identify the patterns. This is how children and adults construct personal meaning. When we are required to learn something that isn't connected to previous knowledge, the process can be very stressful. It feels awkward, inauthentic, and irrelevant and it requires a great deal of controlled attention. Because the learning is not immediately perceived as meaningful, the experience can be resented and frustrating. In short, such inauthentic learning is an 'academic exercise' with no real value outside the classroom or school. It is no accident that irrelevant learning activities are called 'academic' – they were invented in the classroom.

The teachers at the Island School were quick to announce that they were not required to attend these professional learning opportunities, but they felt they needed to in order to be a part of the innovative ethos of the school. In addition, there seemed to be a positive peer group pressure that had come to exist amongst the teachers that also lent to the feeling that attendance was expected, if not actually required.

Organizational ADHD

As educators we may be familiar with the condition of Attention Deficit Hyperactivity Disorder (ADHD) in children or young adults. It manifests it itself in the young person in being impulsive, having difficulty delaying gratification, struggling with anticipating consequences of his or her behavior and having great difficulty maintaining controlled attention on tasks such as learning to read. ADHD is not limited to individuals. On occasion, groups of people or organizations can exhibit the symptoms of ADHD. We call this OADHD (Goleman, 2013), where there are so many competing, unconnected professional stimuli that meaningful learning is negatively affected. We wondered if the Island School was on the brink of OADHD.

When teachers talk about an overload of professional learning, we often equate it to quantity. Teachers at the Island School were quick to point out that they had had seven external consultants in six months. We, however, wondered whether it was not just the quantity of learning experiences that was creating the stress, but rather the seeming disconnectedness of these experiences.

As we listened to the menu of professional learning experiences that the Island School had hosted, we did see possible connections between them. They had had work in ELL, responsive teaching, differentiation, collaboration, Assessment for Learning, and Cognitive Coaching. There were powerful links and connections between the various initiatives; however no one in the school was mediating the connectedness, or making explicit how the various learning experiences dovetailed with each other. No one had taken responsibility for coherence.

Coherence makes visible the big picture; it provides personal meaning for our collective actions; and, it releases energy, builds motivation and commitment and provides glimpses of the most powerful change agent known to humankind – the compelling vision.

How then do school leaders create a culture of coherence?

Appreciative and connective inquiry

School leadership generates coherence by engaging in Connective Inquiry. This is a process that draws from the work of Cognitive Coaching (Costa & Garmston, 2002) and Appreciative Inquiry (Cooperrider & Whitney,

2005). The process is deceptively simple, but is not simplistic. It involves astute, insightful observation, the suspension of judgment, and the mediation of connectedness.

Appreciative inquiry comes to us from the work of David Cooperrider, who in the mid 1980s was involved in an evaluation and analysis of the organizational effectiveness of a medical clinic in Cleveland, Ohio. His task was to observe and interview in order to find what was wrong with respect to the human side of the institution.

Cooperrider embarked on his task only to find that there was a great deal that was positive about the so-called human side of the clinic. This brought about a paradigm shift in his work. Instead of searching for what was *wrong*, Cooperrider began to look for what that was *right*. He started to identify and examine what the strengths were in interpersonal relationships, collaboration and collective innovation. Out of this novel approach came the strategy of Appreciative Inquiry. It is the search for and deconstruction of goodness.

Appreciative Inquiry taps into something that we in education have known for decades (but not always acted upon): the idea that deep and effective learning comes more readily when we focus on student strengths than when we grind on their weaknesses or deficits.

This is illustrated nicely in an anecdote about the star golfer, Tiger Woods. According to the story, Woods' great weakness as a golfer was the trouble that he encountered when faced with sand traps. Bunkers were his Achilles Heel. Whenever he did less than what he considered to be his best in a tournament, the problem lay in escaping from a sand trap.

As a result, Woods decided to focus on his drive. A colleague asked about this apparent inconsistency. "Your weakness is getting out of the sand traps and yet you focus on your drive. What sense does that make?" The response: the drive was Tiger's strength and by improving it, he kept himself out of the sand traps in the first place.

In education we also know that we can achieve vastly more professional growth by focusing on teacher strengths as opposed to their weaknesses. We have been notoriously negligent in deconstructing our professional strengths and successes. We have, instead, used the usual approach to problems.

In traditional, linear problem solving we customarily look at a four-step process:

Define and identify the problem.

Analyze the possible causes.

Develop possible solutions and test them against the environment.

Select the most promising and develop an action plan.

Traditional linear problem-solving can work well for technical problems (repairing automobiles or rectifying electrical faults), but often fall woefully short when we are dealing with highly complex, interdependent, living systems such as schools.

Appreciative Inquiry has a different starting point and process and is neither linear and nor reductionist. The steps include:

Appreciate: Identify what is working well? What releases energy and creativity into the classroom? What specifically contributed to the success of the lesson?

Imagine: What might be? What if...?

Determine: What should be?

Create: What will be?

A culture of encouragement

The essence of Appreciative Inquiry is the search for goodness – the predisposition that there is something effective going on in the vast majority of classrooms and that we need to identify it and rigorously analyze it so that we and others can learn from it. This is not a culture of rose-colored glasses or superficial flattery. It is, however, *a culture of encouragement*. The difference is important. Excessive praise signals that further thinking is unnecessary and when the praise is inauthentic it undermines trust. Encouragement, on the other hand, is future focused. It releases energy for deeper and more complex thinking. Encouragement is the fulcrum that moves insight to implementation.

A friend and colleague of ours, an experienced Head of school, was recruited as the director of a large European school. What she inherited was a toxic culture characterized by emotional bullying: put-downs, meanness and point-scoring. After assessing the situation, she decided to design and implement what she refers to as 'a culture of care', where social sensitivity, emotional intelligence and a focus on relationships are non-negotiables, held in parallel to the school's already rigorous program of academic achievement.

Although it took some time and although there were setbacks, keeping an unwavering view of the goal kept her and the school focused on the long term. A more humane and compassionate culture emerged.

Connective inquiry

However, for Appreciative Inquiry to support the development of a truly compelling collective vision it needs to be connective. It needs to result in coherence. The individual strengths and successes of teachers need to be explicitly linked to the mission and values of the organization. The following assumptions form the foundation of what we are calling Connective Inquiry:

We are all more open to learning when we focus on our strengths and successes.

In most classrooms, we can find effective practice (strategies that work).

In some classrooms, teachers may actually be unaware of their strengths. The identification and recognition of strengths can be both validating and energizing. It can contribute to a culture of encouragement.

The suspension of judgment is the beginning of transformational learning.

Authentic and active listening is crucial for inquiry.

Well-crafted, mediative questions can provide us with alternative perspectives and new insights.

Conversation is our primary means for establishing, sustaining and transforming our personal and professional reality.

When we explicitly connect individual teacher strengths to the mission of the organization, we increase commitment and motivation by building organizational coherence and a culture of encouragement.

Let's pause and examine the last point. Bill is reminded of an occasion when he was part of a series of walk-through observations in the middle school of the International School of Kuala Lumpur. A team of three observers had spent approximately five minutes in four different classes. In two of the classes, the observers had seen teachers using 'wait time' (the teacher had paused between three and five seconds after asking a question before allowing students to answer). The dialogue that followed the walk-through observations included both Appreciative and Connective Inquiry:

Observer #1: "One thing we observed was teacher use of wait time. The students were given time to think before being called upon to respond. What effects might this have had on student responses?"

Teacher #1: "Well, I suppose it gave them think time. I mean some of the kids process more slowly."

Observer #2: "So it kind of leveled the playing field. It gave everyone a chance to contribute."

Teacher #1: "It did. I also find that when wait times is present, shy children are more willing to raise their hands."

Teacher # 2: "I also find that the children's answers are more thoughtful when I give them a bit of wait time."

Observer #3: "So, in a way, the silence conveys the message to the students that the question is worthy of deep thought."

Teacher #2: "I hadn't thought about the message that silence might give. That's interesting."

Teacher #3: "But it is hard in the middle of a lesson to remember to give students wait time. I know it's a good idea, I just don't always remember to do it."

Observer #1: (redirecting the question back to Teacher #1): "What might be some of your values as an educator that underpin the use of wait time?"

Teacher #1: "I suppose that I want my class to be a thoughtful place. I want students to be engaged in thinking. So I guess it's only natural that we would give them time to think."

Observer #2: "So a strong value for you is to develop higher order thinking skills in your students."

Teacher #1: "And different kids need different processing times."

Teacher #3: "So, wait time is a form of differentiation."

Teacher #2: "In a way, it allows us to personalize learning."

Observer # 3: "You're seeing some connections."

Teacher #1: "Actually, I hadn't thought about wait time as a way of differentiating, but I suppose in a way it is. It allows all students to enter the question at their own readiness level. Some may be at a quite concrete level others may have more sophisticated and abstract thoughts. I learned about 'wait time' during our Cognitive Coaching training. I guess you can use the coaching strategies for differentiation."

Observer #2: "And 'wait time' is linked directly to our trans-disciplinary standards."

Teacher #3: "In what way?"

Observer #1: "To the school's mission of developing independent, critical thinkers".

Distinguishing between strategies and goals

A very common obstacle to learning coherence in schools is confusion between strategies and goals. This is more widespread than any of us would like to acknowledge and is worthy of our attention. This work comes to us from Nick Bowley, a veteran international educator and school leader (Bowley 2008, personal communication).

Nick was the Head of an international school in China during the outbreak of Severe Acute Respiratory Syndrome (SARS) from 2002 to 2004. The disease originated in Guangdong Province in China but quickly spread to Hong Kong, Vietnam, Thailand, Taiwan, and Singapore. The spread of the often-lethal disease was accompanied by alarmist media reports, government initiated travel restrictions and in some cases mandatory quarantine for suspected cases of SARS.

Naturally, schools in the affected areas took the outbreak very seriously and implemented a number of preventative measures such as regular, compulsory hand washing, monitoring student and staff temperatures at the entrance gate, and periodic disinfecting of classroom areas and furniture. So far, so good. However, as the disease evolved so did the advice and recommendations from the experts at the Centers for Disease Control (CDC) and the World Health Organization (WHO). One week, disinfecting desktops was to take place twice a day; the next week it was to take place hourly.

In this highly stressful and anxious environment, the changes in preventative procedures had a negative effect on some of the teaching staff. They interpreted the changes as evidence that the school leadership didn't actually know what it was doing and consequently weren't 'in charge' of the situation. In such an environment terrifying and frightening rumors abounded. Nick decided to take the proverbial bull by the horns.

He called the staff together and explained to them the critical distinction between goals and strategies. A goal was an overarching and sustainable outcome that the school community was committed to. In the case of the SARS epidemic, the school's goals were to maintain a safe and healthy environment of children and staff and, at the same time, continue the challenging program of study as much as possible. These goals were unlikely to change. However, the strategies that supported the goal were highly fluid. These could change on a week-to-week basis or even daily as new information about the epidemic became available. The distinction between goals and strategies lowered the stress level and helped curb the rumors and gossip. The distinction provided coherence.

Measuring what really matters

Another area in which we often see confusion between goals and strategies is in measuring or assessing what truly matters. Most high quality schools go through regular accreditation processes. The cycle includes an in-depth self-study that the school undertakes that is followed by an onsite examination by a visiting accreditation team. The visiting team spends a number of days at the school, confirming the school's self-study and writing a comprehensive report that includes both commendations and recommendations. The recommendations are then compiled into a school-wide action plan. However, often confusion between goals and strategies can lead to a false sense of accomplishment.

For example, let's assume that the accreditation report includes a recommendation that the teachers at School X need to incorporate greater differentiation in their classrooms. The school leadership recognizes that the teachers may need support in this goal so that they contract with an external consultant to provide training in differentiation.

The training, however, is not the goal. It is a strategy. The completion of the differentiation training is NOT the accomplishment of the goal. Talking about an issue is not necessarily the same as addressing it. When assessing the effectiveness of the Action Plan, we need to measure what really matters. This requires us to distinguish between goals and strategies.

Verbs and nouns

The researcher Marc Prensky (2012), father of the phrase 'digital native', provides some useful clarification when it comes to distinguishing between goals and strategies. Rapid change has been the norm in the field of educational technology for many years. This break-neck pace of change, coupled with the fact that students are often more facile with technology than their teachers, can produce stress and considerable confusion.

In a keynote address at the European Council of International Schools Teachers' Conference, Prensky displayed a large T-chart, similar to the one below. In the left hand column he had verbs and in the right hand column he had nouns. According to him, the verbs represent the enduring goals of education and schooling. These are unlikely to change. The nouns in the right-hand column represent the technological strategies that we might use in order to accomplish our goals. The nouns are highly suspectible to change. When we distinguish between verbs and nouns (goals and strategies) in the confusing and rapidly changing field of educational technology we develop learning coherence.

Verbs	Nouns
Communicate	Internet
Research	Google
Analyze	Blog
Listen	Wiki
Evaluate	Email
Predict	Twitter
Calculate	Facebook
Practice	Skype
Empathize	Facetime
Create	iMovie

Wrapping Up

Teacher self-supervision is all about teacher self-directed learning. Such learning thrives in a culture of coherence: a school culture in which there are strong and explicit connections between actions, decisions, behaviors, initiatives and the core values and shared beliefs of the organization. One of the most important tasks of leadership is to provide such coherence, to support teachers and students in connecting the dots. This is leadership through Appreciative and Connective Inquiry: leadership by posing powerful questions that generate energy and focused thinking, reveal hidden and unexamined assumptions and open new possibilities for action.

References

Brooks, J.G. & Brooks, M.G. (1999). In search of understanding: The case for the constructivist classroom. Alexandria, VA:Association for Supervision and Curriculum Development.

Cooperrider, D. & Whitney, D. (2005). Appreciative inquiry: A positive revolution in change. San Francisco: Berrett-Koehler.

Costa, A. & Garmston, R. (2002). Cognitive coaching: A foundation for renaissance Schools. Norwood, MA: Christopher-Gordon Publishers.

Goleman, D. (2013). Focus: The hidden driver of excellence. New York: Harpercollins.

Forster, E.M. (2002). *Howards End*. Mineola, NY: Dover Publications.

Prensky, M. (2012). Keynote address at the European Council of International Schools, Nice, France.

Chapter 7

It's all about differentiation

Differentiation in education, or personalized learning as it is called in Britain, has a long history. There is a story, told to us by a Burmese teacher in Yangon, about how several disciples of the Lord Buddha came to him to complain that their students were very slow in learning how to meditate. Buddha was silent for several moments.

"Have you looked at your students' sandals?" Buddha asked.

"Their sandals!" the disciples exclaimed. "What have their sandals to do with meditation?"

Buddha smiled and began to explain. If the student's sandals were well worn in the front, it would suggest that student had the habit of rushing into things. The student might be impulsive, energetic or overly enthusiastic. These could be strengths in learning but only when coupled with perseverance and thoughtfulness.

If a student's sandals were well worn at the back, it might suggest that he was a hesitant learner. The student might be naturally reticent or shy or perhaps lacking in self-confidence. This student might need encouragement, experiences with success and moral support.

If the students' sandals were well worn in the middle, it might suggest that the student was well balanced and a more middle-of-the-road approach was appropriate.

Buddha's metaphorical message to his disciples was that students learn in different ways depending on many different factors. When teachers understand their students as learners, we open up a multitude of opportunities for student learning, achievement and success. When school leaders understand the development and readiness levels of their teachers, adult professional learning is greatly accelerated.

If differentiated learning makes sense in the classroom for students, why would it not make sense for teachers?

Arguably the most prevalent, and in some arenas controversial, teacher evaluation system in the United States at this point in time is the Charlotte Danielson Framework for Teaching Evaluation Instrument (2013). The Danielson Framework attempts to establish a common language (with clear and accessible definitions of jargon terms) and a common understanding of excellence. It includes rubrics in four domains of teaching and learning together with 'critical attributes' and snapshot learning and teaching exemplars. However, its implementation has been problematic and a plethora of lawsuits hover on the horizon.

In our minds, there are two major issues with the Danielson Framework. The first problem is that it is monolithic – one size fits all teachers; the second issue is that the evaluation continues the pernicious tradition of being external to self. In the introduction to the Framework Danielson writes:

> In most classrooms students don't take an active role in their own learning, nor do they (respectfully) challenge the thinking of their classmates. All of this will represent a major departure and therefore a major challenge for many teachers. (p.5)

It appears from this that one of Danielson's goals is for students to become self-directed, independent thinkers. We applaud this goal, but query how it is possible unless we also support teachers in also becoming self-directed, independent thinkers. While paying lip service to student self-directedness, the emphasis on external, one-size-fits-all teacher evaluation perpetuates the notion that education is something that happens to you, rather than something you actively engage in.

In an elementary classroom the primary architect of differentiated instruction and personalized learning is the teacher. Primary school children are simply not developmentally ready to do so for themselves. As students move into middle and high schools, we expect them to take increasing responsibility for their own learning. We expect them to explore their own zone of proximal development and set challenging, personalized goals for themselves. We expect greater and more accurate self-assessment. If teachers are ultimately responsible for this evolving independence in students, why would we assume that they are incapable of applying it to themselves?

Equality *vs* equity

Traditional teacher evaluation systems assume that one supervision protocol will be appropriate for all. Equality (treating everyone in exactly the same way) is equated with objectivity and the appearance of fairness. In reality, we know that all teachers do not have the same learning needs. It is absurd to assume they do. Treating everyone in exactly the same manner creates merely the illusion of fairness. We prefer to employ the concept of *equity*, that is providing teachers with what they need for success in the classroom and success in their own self-directed learning. This will be different at different levels of professional and personal development, but is at the heart of transformational learning.

Objectivity and subjectivity

The West has a long intellectual tradition of dialectical thinking, of setting up contradictory ideas for logical argumentation. It is the basis of much of our philosophical thinking, the experimental sciences, mathematics and our precedent based systems of jurisprudence. These processes rely on the formulation of pure types that may or may not have great utility in the rather messy and confused world that most of us actually inhabit. Let's take the example of objectivity and subjectivity.

Most of us think of an *objective approach* as one that is not influenced by emotion or personal prejudice; one that is based upon observable phenomena. We commonly use the word *objective* as a synonym for fair, detached, dispassionate, evenhanded, unbiased, and impersonal. In this context, we generally consider that an objective approach has a positive connotation. We generally consider an objective approach to an issue or problem to be constructive.

On the other hand, subjectivity has recently got a bad name. We associate a *subjective approach* to an issue with prejudice, bias, and personal opinion that is divorced from observable data. We tend to dismiss subjectivity as idiosyncratic. *That's just your opinion.* However, this may be a simplistic understanding of subjectivity.

We suggest that one approach is not necessarily better than another. In fact, we would argue that both objective and subjective approaches may complement each other. They may be interdependent polarities that need to be carefully managed. If the proverbial pendulum swings too far in either direction, meaning-making suffers.

Objective and subjective approaches to meaning-making have different starting points. The objective approach begins with observable data and then proceeds to analysis and interpretation. The subjective approach begins with an idea or concept in the mind and then proceeds to data gathering, analysis and potential validation.

Subjectivity may involve intuition – that way of knowing that gives us a 'sense of something'. For example, a teacher may not know what is wrong with the social dynamic of the class, but she has a 'sense' that something has happened that is producing collective pre-occupation. When we anchor subjectivity (our inferences) in observable data we avoid capriciousness and move towards sound professional judgment.

Given the complexity of teaching and learning, we would argue that balancing objectivity and subjectivity is a key element in effective self-supervision. Perhaps the strongest argument for differentiated teacher supervision comes not only from the fact that teachers are a very diverse group of learners, but also that they develop over time. The professional self is and should be a moving target.

Self as process, not product

We are coming to learn a great deal about our sense of self – what we hold to be our unique identity. For many of us there is a strong temptation to view our identity as something fixed and immutable: a permanent, and half hidden statue that resides at the very core of our being. We talk about 'exploring our identity' as though it were a fixed topography or 'coming to find our self' as though we were archeologists unearthing a timeless artifact.

While this vision of self fosters the illusion of stability and certainty and may be comforting, psychologists and neuroscientists are increasingly suggesting that self may be a fluid process, not a product (Erickson, 1950, May, 1953, Kegan, 1982). In other words, my identity will change over time. At 65, Bill is not the same person as he was at 19. (Ochan says: *Thank God*). The self evolves and is influenced by many factors: our environment, culture, gender, relationships, employment, assumptions and belief systems, *etc.*

The idea that adults continue to develop throughout their lifetime is a relatively new one. Developmental theory in education comes to us from the work of Erik Erikson and Jean Piaget. But because both focused on the work of children and young adults, we came to assume that most cognitive and emotional growth was complete around the age of 20. By 30, we erroneously assumed, we were a finished product.

We can remember being told with great authority that no new brain cells were produced after the late teenage years. Yes, we could learn new things, but we really couldn't change who we were or how intelligent we are. We now know that this is simply not true (Dweck, 2008; Doidge, 2007). Neurogenesis is ongoing and adults have the capacity to continue to develop cognitively, emotionally and spiritually throughout their lifetimes.

Our identity is our primary meaning-making interface with the external world; it is the narrative that we tell about who we are; and it is the filter that we use to make sense of the world. Having said that, identity is also fluid and constantly changing, but is critically influential in determining our decision-making and behavior.

How is the evolving self connected to differentiated teacher supervision?

We believe that teachers at different stages of their cognitive and emotional development will have differing professional and personal needs. If school leaders are able to understand and appreciate the developmental and readiness level of teachers, the leaders will be more effective in supporting teacher self-directed learning.

Drago-Seversen (2009) writes about optimal adult learning taking place in healthy 'holding environments' where the appropriate level of supports and challenges are present. In order to identify those appropriate supports and challenges, we need to understand the developmental level of the teacher. Better yet, individual teachers need to do so for themselves.

We also need to understand that there is a direct and powerful correlation between the intellectual developmental level of the teacher and the complexity of the cognitive functioning of his/her students. Teachers who make sense out of the world in more complex ways will generate deeper conceptual thinking in their students than those who have simpler, more rule-bound and dichotomous mental models. Costa, Garmston and Zimmerman (2014) write:

> Higher-level intellectual functioning teachers produce higher-level intellectually functioning students... Characteristic of such teachers is their ability to empathize, to symbolize experience and to act in accordance with a disciplined commitment to human values. They employ a greater range of instructional strategies, elicit more conceptual responses from students and produce higher achieving students who are more cooperative and involved in their work. (p.13)

Differentiated supervision of teachers is based upon a developmental stance. In other words, we believe that none of us are finished products and that with focused attention and mindfulness we can grow and improve our practice. This is the essence of what Carol Dweck (2008) refers to as a 'growth mindset'.

Traditional systems of teacher evaluation inhibit teacher learning and improvement in two important ways. First, while paying lip service to professional growth, the practices of such systems of teacher evaluation actually create obstacles to adult learning. They foster a sense of comparison and competition between teachers. Punitive evaluation systems – virtually all of them – also perceive revealed deficits in teaching practice as a weakness and tacitly encourage teachers to either hide aspects of their work that they may feel less secure about or externalize the blame. This breeds privacy of practice and a pervasive sense of professional isolation. Michael Fullan (2001) perceives teacher isolation as the enemy of improvement.

> Leaders must create environments in which individuals expect to have their personal ideas and practices subjected to the scrutiny of their colleagues, and in which groups expect to have their shared conceptions of practice subjected to the scrutiny of individuals. Privacy of practice produces isolation; isolation is the enemy of improvement. (p.20)

The second way that traditional systems of teacher evaluation inhibit adult learning is through confidentiality. In many such systems, the actual summative written appraisal of the teacher is considered a confidential document with access limited to the teacher and the supervisor. This confidentiality further promotes the idea that teaching practice is essentially private practice and codifies teacher isolation. When we de-privatize practice, we actively search for goodness and deconstruct it; we analyze feedback with colleagues; we deliberately and judiciously set personal learning goals; we engage in mutual reflection and accordingly we build cultures with a fabric of trust. It is then that we promote adult self-directed learning.

Stages of adult development

In order for teachers to engage in meaningful learning that leads to enhanced student learning there needs to be a match between the development level of the individual teacher and his or her 'holding environment', for instance the cognitive and emotional supports and challenges that are provided (Drago-Seversen, 2009). This match of developmental level and holding environment is the essence of differentiated teacher supervision.

Harvard psychologist Robert Kegan (1982) has developed a theory of adult development that has significant implications for teacher learning. Unlike some earlier psychologists, Kegan does not see mental and emotional growth ending in late adolescence. He sees human development as a lifelong, dynamic process.

Kegan's Constructive-Developmental Theory is based on how adults make meaning of the world around them. His theory holds that as we grow cognitively and emotionally, the ways that we construct meaning become more and more complex. His research suggests that the ways in which we construct meaning are not necessarily associated with gender, age, or life phase.

Meaning-making is developmental and Kegan suggests to us that there are four developmental stages of adult life: instrumental; socializing; self-authoring; and self-transforming. Each of these developmental stages incorporates the former into its new, more expansive meaning-making system. Although this theory appears as a series of levels or hierarchy, one way of knowing is not necessarily better than another and Kegan stresses that an appropriate developmental stage matches the level of complexity of the environment. While the real world is rarely inhabited by pure types, Kegan's model provides a valuable structure for thinking about teacher supervision.

The instrumental teacher

The teacher at the instrumental stage of knowing has a very basic and defined orientation to the world. Meaning-making is focused on achieving his or her own concrete needs and desires. An instrumental knower cannot take on the perspective of another person fully and empathy is very limited. Colleagues are perceived as either helpers or hinderers to getting one's own needs met. Teachers at an instrumental level tend to be opportunistic; they look to realize their goals in any way possible. Personal need fulfillment may trump ethics and morality. They can perceive other people as agents to be used and often have a strong need to control or direct the outcome of activities.

People at the instrumental stage of knowing often engage in what Edward de Bono (1992) refers to as 'rock logic'. They believe in and need right and wrong answers. They are not comfortable until they have a 'right' way to think and 'right' way to act. They generally want to learn 'the rules' – whether the rules dictate how to teach a lesson, collaborate with colleagues, or design unit plans. They tend to dismiss inquiry, preferring direct instruction. *Just tell me the best way to do it.* Instrumental knowers have little appreciation of shades of gray, irony or paradoxes and virtually no tolerance for ambiguity.

Because instrumental knowers are not yet capable of meaningful empathy, they tend to make ineffective teachers and in many cases are not attracted to the profession. However, the inherent complexities of teaching and learning can make school a frustrating place for the instrumental teacher and this discomfort can manifest itself in rigidity (an over-reliance on rules and regulations), resistance to change and staffroom negativity. When confronted with an adult learning opportunity, we might hear: "Why can't the administration leave us alone to get on with what we have been trained to do?"

An instrumental teacher needs a holding environment that includes supports (precise direction, external organization, explicit guidance, step-by-step instructions and a focus on concrete, behavioral craftsmanship).

The instrumental holding environment also needs to include challenges (opportunities to extend empathy, situations that require multiple perspective taking, and encouragement of greater consciousness – how is my participation affecting others in the group?). Instrumental teachers often benefit from artfully naïve questions (Garmston & Wellman, 2009) such as 'Is this a matter of principle or practice?'

The socializing teacher

With respect to the general population, the socializing stage of development is by far the largest and includes most older adolescents and adults. The individual at the socializing stage of development has the capacity to think abstractly and is able to respond to the needs of others; s/he can identify with and internalize the feelings of others. However, socializing individuals are driven by the opinions, expectations and perceptions of others; their needs are externally defined by their peer group. Loyalty, group cohesion and stability are of paramount importance.

For the socializing knower, interpersonal conflict can be experienced as a threat to group cohesion; thus the socializing knower avoids conflict because it is a risk to the relationship. They find providing critical feedback extremely difficult and can be paralyzed when faced with making unpopular decisions. Rooke and Torbert (2005) refer to leaders at this stage as 'Diplomats' who obey group norms (without real examination) and tend not to rock the boat.

The strengths of the socializing individual is that he or she can provide cohesion to groups, attend to the needs of others, but often is unable to distinguish between positive teams and negative dysfunctional ones. Loyalty is a paramount virtue to the socializing teacher often at the expense of critical thinking or ethical considerations.

The socializing teacher finds validation and meaning in the approval and acceptance of others. They look to be affirmed and validated by students, colleagues, and supervisors. Specifically, the socializing teacher will seek to win the approval of higher status colleagues. In extreme cases, some socializing teachers appear addicted to praise and external appreciation and when such approbation is absent, these teachers go into a form of accolade withdrawal – in which the adulation vacuum is perceived to be filling with criticism.

While socializing teachers want and need external validation (praise from colleagues or the principal), they often do not want to be so much in the spotlight that they stand out from other teachers. The socializing teacher may also be reluctant to accept positions of responsibility that require making potentially difficult or unpopular decisions.

When socializing individuals are appointed to senior positions of leadership, the situation can become even more problematic as they will tend to ignore conflict and find it virtually impossible to provide challenging feedback. They are usually very poor at initiating school improvement plans because they perceive such changes will inevitably involve much dreaded conflict.

Kegan (1982) stresses that it is difficult for an individual to develop to a greater level of complexity than his or her surrounding peer group. We know that the teacher performance is profoundly influenced by the quality of peers (Jackson & Bruegmann, 2009). Accordingly, developmentally diverse groups provide many opportunities of peer learning.

Because of the strong service ethic that is associated with teaching, many socializing individuals are drawn to the profession – as a generalization – probably more so to primary than secondary schools. The healthy holding environment for socializing teachers includes both supports and challenges. The supports might involve paying attention to them, carving out time to build relationships, demonstrations of personal regard, authentic listening, paraphrasing, and expressions of encouragement (not necessarily the same as praise).

The challenges would involve the socializing teacher in developing a greater sense of autonomy and individualization. They may benefit from probing questions regarding internal motivation that is linked to emerging values and beliefs or from reflective questions that illuminate a greater sense of efficacy and empowerment.

Socializing teachers may also benefit from public recognition when they do take the courageous step and place their own ideas on the table. It can also be useful to support the socializing teacher in perceiving the difference between assertiveness and aggression and between cognitive conflict (healthy debate over ideas and issues) and affective conflict (destructive, personalized conflict).

The self-authoring teacher

Self-authoring teachers have developed internalized values and corresponding sets of rules for their own behavior; they are not dependent on others for meaning-making, evaluation or esteem. They tend to be self-guided, self-evaluative, and self-motivated. They can be efficacious and task-oriented, and tend to gravitate in schools towards positions of leadership and responsibility. Self-authoring teachers are self-motivated and pursue continuous improvement and efficiency. They take considerable pride in their performance in the classroom and genuinely want their students to achieve and succeed.

Self-authoring teachers tend to be the more experienced and mature members of faculty with a well-developed content knowledge base and relatively large repertoire of instructional pedagogy. They often place a considerable degree of emphasis on craftsmanship, set challenging goals for themselves and are in the process of becoming master teachers.

Rooke and Torbert (2005) refer to this developmental stage as the 'Experts'. 'Experts try to exercise control by perfecting their knowledge, both in their professional and personal lives. Exercising watertight thinking is extremely important to Experts...' (p.6). The pursuit of such watertight thinking can result in professional rigidity and, occasionally, they can be perceived by colleagues as perfectionists. They may not have well developed interpersonal skills and emotional intelligence may not be highly valued. In addition, some may perceive collaboration as a waste of time.

However, self-authoring teachers can develop relationship orientation and can learn social sensitivity and emotional intelligence (Powell & Kusuma-Powell, 2010). When this occurs we see the emergence of what Rooke and Torbert (2009) call the Self-Authoring Achiever. These individuals can manage their feelings and emotions and are able to discuss their internal states. They can be other-centered and sensitive to the social interactions of groups. Self-authoring achievers have the capacity for reflection on their multiple roles as teachers, leaders, parents, partners and citizens. Competence, achievement, and responsibility are the uppermost concerns of people who make meaning in this way.

Self-authoring achievers have internalized a series of values and beliefs about teaching and learning, and their professional behavior is guided by those values and beliefs. They are open to feedback and realize that many of the conflicts of everyday life may be the result of differences in perception and interpretation.

However, the self-authoring teacher may also be quirky and eccentric. They may ignore rules and regulations that they regard as irrelevant, which may bring them into conflict with school leaders or colleagues. Prescribed curriculum may be bemoaned as inhibiting creativity and what are perceived as 'educational fads' may be greeted with skepticism. The self-authoring achiever is self-directed and self-evaluating and may actually find external direction and evaluation (including praise) de-motivating.

The healthy holding environment for a self-authoring teacher includes both supports and challenges. The supports might focus upon opportunities for leadership and mentoring of less experienced teachers. They may appreciate the sense of accomplishment that comes with the achievement of a challenging goal – particularly when the accomplishment is connected to their sense of mission. Self-authoring teachers are often engaged in exploring what may be a relatively new found sense of integrity; the congruence between values and actions may be a source of motivation for them and they may appreciate colleagues drawing explicit connections between their beliefs and their behavior and decision-making.

Challenges for self-authoring teachers can reside in the domain of flexibility (being able to see the perspectives of others), consciousness (mindfulness) and interdependence. Many self-authoring teachers have already become reflective on their craftsmanship and may find it useful to extend the reflection to include the interpersonal and intrapersonal realms. They may benefit from exploring what may be going on internally for others (students in their classroom or colleagues) and in developing the detachment necessary to explore their own internal states. Self-authoring teachers sometimes benefit greatly from deliberate training in coaching, facilitation and collaboration skills.

The self-transforming teacher

Kegan (1982) posits that the self-transforming stage is ideal for a world that embraces complexity, chaos and interactive and adaptive systems. Since few schools actively embrace these attributes, self-transforming teachers tend to be relatively rare. Self-transforming individuals are able to see beyond the limits of their own internal systems. They appreciate that perceptions are not the same as external reality and are open to multiple and even contradictory interpretations.

These are individuals who are constantly inviting themselves to see things in a different way: *Are there other ways for us to interpret the situation?* Self-transforming teachers search out the assumptions that lie beneath our beliefs, analyze them and identify the implications of those assumptions. Self-transforming individuals are able to tolerate and appreciate ambiguity and uncertainty. They tend to see grey instead of black and white. They reconsider and reconstruct what at first seemed clear and straightforward. They move from the known to the unknown, from certainty to uncertainty and their lives are rich in small and large ironies.

Self-transforming teachers may be misunderstood by colleagues at less complex stages of development. They may be perceived as eccentric, difficult or contrary. Sometimes they are accused of questioning simply for the sake of questioning. Their active curiosity may be frustrating to task-orientated individuals who value product over process.

The self-transforming teacher has highly developed internal values and beliefs and is able to integrate these with a sense of purpose that is larger than self. Autonomy and integration are seen as polarities to be managed. In other words, individualism and collectivism are perceived as interdependent; being true to one's self is not necessarily opposed to being a subordinate member of a community or group; leadership and followership form a seamless dance. Self-transforming individuals question and challenge dichotomous thinking, which may bring them into conflict with colleagues at less complex stages of development.

The self-transforming teacher is less constrained by organizational taboos and will often raise such 'forbidden' topics or address directly the elephant in the room. This may not always be appreciated by colleagues. Perhaps the most distinctive feature of self-transforming individuals is that they are motivated by a desire to develop deeper understanding. On occasion, this deeper understanding can become a compelling vision.

Self-transforming teachers are often intuitively aware of the developmental stages of colleagues and are able to provide them with appropriate 'holding environments'. In other words they provide appropriate supports (psychological safety) and challenges for the specific stage of development. In this they can become powerful transformational leaders. With social sensitivity and emotional intelligence, self-transforming teachers can become very effective change agents.

Summary of Kegan's Stages of Adult Development[1]

Instrumental	Socializing	Self-Authoring	Self-Transforming
Many adolescents and some adults.	Some older adolescents and most adults.	Fewer than half of adults.	Few adults, usually after the age of 40.
Are motivated by concrete needs, interests and wishes	Can internalize the feelings of other and are guided by them.	Have developed an internal set of rules.	See beyond the limits of their own systems.
Oriented to self-interests.	Able to abstract and respond to needs other than their own.	Internal governing system for decision-making and conflict resolution.	Perceives grey as opposed to black and white
Are rule based. Looking for the 'right' answer, the 'right' way to do things.	The expectations of others define what I want.	Not dependent on others for evaluation or esteem.	Devoted to something beyond themselves.
Decisions are based on self-interest.	Decisions are based on what others think.	Decisions are based on internal values and beliefs.	Decisions take into account complexity. Individual is able to look across systems.
Guiding questions: *What's in it for me? Will I get punished?*	Ideal for tribal village model where loyalty to the group is paramount.	Ideal for a diverse and mobile world focused on science and the search for truth.	Ideal for a world that rejects objectivity and embraces subjectivity, complexity, chaos and interactive systems.

What might differentiation in teacher supervision look like?

Many schools are realizing that the traditional one-size-fits-all supervision model is simply not working and are struggling to put in place a constructive, humane, learning focused alternative. Here we are drawing upon the work that has been undertaken in the International School of Kuala Lumpur and the International School of Brussels, both of which

1 Adapted from Leading Adult Learning (2010) by E. Drago-Severson, Corwin Press and Becoming an Emotionally Intelligent Teacher (2010) by W. Powell & O. Kusuma-Powell, Corwin Press and The OIQ Factor: Raising the organizational intelligence of your school by W. Powell & O. Kusuma-Powell, (2013) John Catt Educational.

have endeavored to differentiate teacher supervision to meet the specific needs of differing stages of professional development.

At the International School of Kuala Lumpur, Bill worked with the leadership team and faculty to implement a differentiated system of teacher supervision that included four levels or stages (Figure 3), described below. The design process was collaborative with teachers, principals and Bill working together to define the levels, identify the supports and challenges, and the ways in which teachers would demonstrate self-directed learning. However, there was a non-negotiable on the table from the very start of the collaborative process: the levels of supervision would NOT attract financial reward. There would be no stipend associated with the levels: this would not be a way to disguise merit pay.

Differentiated supervision level one: intense assistance

The intense assistance level is reserved for the ineffective or marginal teacher who appears unable to improve without direct, external intervention. In this situation, the teacher does not appear to have an internal locus of control and at this stage of development self-direction is unlikely. The goal of intense assistance is one of the following:

1. To support the teacher in meeting the teaching standards of the school in a relatively short period of time (six to eight weeks), or;
2. To document a case for removing the teacher from the classroom in a relatively short period of time (six to eight weeks).

If care and due diligence are taken in the hiring process, intense assistance cases will be few and far between. In most international schools, only 1-2% of teachers will warrant this status. The role of the supervisor (usually the principal or assistant principal) is that of an external evaluator and consultant. There is high directive behavior on the part of the supervisor who uses classroom observations, unit and lesson plan analysis to gather data, provide high quality feedback and monitor that the feedback is being implemented in the classroom.

Supervising such teachers is very labor intensive and principals need to deliberately determine how much time and energy they are prepared to invest. We would state again that we believe it is a reasonable expectation for teachers to be self-directed. If they are not, it may be that they are in the wrong profession. Some adults simply should not be teachers – they may lack the intelligence, social sensitivity or dispositions. It is not the work of principals to 'water the rocks'.

In many cases the outcome of intense assistance status will be determined by the type of learning required (knowledge, skills and/or attitude) and the degree to which the teacher accepts responsibility for his or her own learning. Informational learning can take place quite rapidly; skill development and mastery takes longer; and modification in attitudes may take even longer.

Differentiated supervision level two: initial direct

Initial direct supervision is reserved for either new teachers to the school, young and inexperienced teachers, interns, and those teachers requesting it when taking on new teaching responsibilities (for example, changing a grade level or subject area.)

Generally speaking, the caseload of initial direct supervision should be no more than 10-15% of the faculty. The goal of initial direct supervision is to support the teacher in developing sufficient self-direction so that he or she can move into transitional supervision and take responsibility for his or her own self-assessment, goal setting, monitoring of progress, reflection and learning.

The role of the supervisor is that of mentor and can be fulfilled by the principal, assistant principal, head of department, team leader or any experienced faculty member. The mentor engages in high directive and high supportive behavior. Initially there is a considerable degree of guidance and direction accompanied by significant encouragement and moral support.

Depending on the needs of the teacher, the mentor will navigate between consultancy, evaluation, collaboration and coaching. The Mentor will employ classroom observation, unit and lesson plan analysis, and structured planning and reflecting conversations. The general trajectory of mentoring is from external to internal direction.

Accordingly, the mentor will find herself moving during the course of the year from consulting to coaching (from initially offering advice and suggestions toward a stance more aligned to supporting the deep thinking of the mentee).

At ISKL the understanding was that all teachers were expected to move from initial direct supervision to transitional supervision within their first 12 months at the school. This was in keeping with the expectation that all teachers would be self-directed learners.

Differentiated supervision level three: transitional

The goal of the transitional level of supervision is for the teacher to take full responsibility for his or her professional learning and ongoing improvement. At ISKL, this was by far the largest number of faculty members, approximately 60-75% of the teachers. The assumption at the transitional level was that the teacher had internalized motivation and responsibility for professional learning.

The teacher was equipped to self-assess his/her performance (often with the assistance of a colleague or critical friend), set meaningful and challenging goals, monitor progress and engage in structured reflection – often in conversation with colleagues. There was also the expectation at the transitional level that the teacher would be a consumer of educational research. He or she would read articles and attempt to stay abreast of developments in their fields.

The teacher at the transitional level of supervision demonstrates ongoing self-directed learning by engaging in peer observation and coaching, micro-teaching activities, and participation in structured reflection with colleagues.

The supervisor at the transitional level is primarily a coach, in that s/he is a mediator of adult learning. We take the word 'mediator' from the work of Cognitive Coaching. It refers to an individual who supports and facilitates the deep thinking of another person. The meditative coach withholds judgment, advice and recommendations, confident that teachers at this level have the necessary internal resources to do their own planning, reflecting and problem resolving.

The coach does, however, use the essential pattern of pausing, paraphrasing, pausing, and inquiry or probing for specificity in order to support the deep critical thinking of the teacher. As the teacher develops greater self-direction, the need for external direction diminishes and we see emerging increased craftsmanship, consciousness, flexibility, efficacy and interdependence.

Differentiated supervision level four: leadership

In every school there will be a group of teachers who not only take on responsibility for their own professional learning, but also extend this responsibility to their colleagues. Leadership level supervision recognizes the roles these teachers play in initiating professional learning activities for colleagues. The goal of leadership level supervision is to create and nurture a culture of shared learning. It is essentially other-centered and the teacher is a leader of adult learning, actively engaged in sharing new knowledge and insights. This is the teacher who is pro-actively sharing professional articles or leading workshops. The leadership level teacher not only consumes research findings and disseminates them, but also generates new knowledge through his or her own action research.

Teachers at both the transitional and leadership levels exhibit what Costa, Garmston and Zimmerman (2014) refer to as 'learning agility'. This is the capacity to accept responsibility and adapt when faced with new challenges. Learning agility manifests itself in how teachers learn from mistakes, how they demonstrate honest and deep reflection and self-modification.

The 'supervisor' at this level is not actually a supervisor in any traditional sense. The principal provides little or no direction or support, because it is simply not needed. Here we are dealing with a self-reliant achiever. (In fact, if the principal does provide direction or support, it may be resented as either micro-managing or patronizing.) Instead, the principals serve as a coach in terms of providing structured opportunities for the teacher to plan, reflect and problem resolve.

As with the transitional level, the coach withholds judgement and advice (commendations and recommendations) and uses the essential mediative pattern of pausing, paraphrasing, pausing and inquiry or probing for specificity to help the teacher become more resourceful. The principal maintains faith in the teacher's capacity to think for himself, confident that teachers at the leadership level have the wherewithal to self-assess, self-monitor and self-modify. The principal may also become a collaborator with the leadership level teacher in planning and executing professional learning opportunities.

In her research on cognitive coaching our colleague, Jenny Edwards, has noted that the paradigm shift from the traditional teacher evaluator to the identity of coach/mediator is frequently accompanied by increased professional motivation and fulfillment. Mediators experience greater feelings of power and satisfaction in observing others and become more self-reliant and resourceful (Edwards, 2005, cited in Costa, Garmston & Zimmerman). This truly represents the highest level of leadership in which the goal is to build leadership capacity in others.

Structured professional self-assessment: what does it look like?

We know from our experiences in the classroom that it is not enough to simply tell students to self-assess. Without guidance and training they will not know how to engage in it and the results will be meaningless. The same is true for teachers.

Many schools ask teachers to set annual goals for themselves. On the surface, this would seem to be a reasonable thing to do. However, without meaningful and rigorous professional self-assessment, teacher goal setting is often a superficial and vapid exercise and has no real influence on instructional improvement.

In order to be meaningful, self-assessment needs to be structured around explicit and commonly understood and accepted learning standards. These are often presented in the form of a rubric or an evolutionary continuum. We prefer the concept of a continuum as the levels of development are all presented in the positive (they reflect the *readiness* level of the teacher as opposed to the *ability*).

The levels of a traditional rubric may include: unsatisfactory, basic, proficient and distinguished. No one wants to label themselves as 'unsatisfactory' or 'basic'. The levels of an evolutionary continuum might include: exploring it, growing it, living it, and transforming it (NFI, 2013). The assumption here is that of a growth mindset – the more we practice something, the better we become at it. Everyone starts as a beginner and with practice becomes an intermediate and with more practice, advanced.

Costa, Garmston and Zimmerman (2014) present the outline for what they refer to as a Calibrating Conversation[2]. The purpose of a Calibrating Conversation is to

2 The Calibrating conversation forms part of the training provided in the Coacnitive Coaching Seminars. Please see www.thinkingcollaborative.com

engage teachers in assessing their own performance related to a set of standards or external criteria, so that, rather than being the recipients of an evaluation, they share responsibility for self-assessing, and then self-prescribing personal responses to the assessment. (p.17)

We believe the impact of the Calibrating Conversation comes out of the combination of self-assessment and self-prescription. This internal intersection produces the energy and drive for actual implementation.

Figure 3: Differentiated Supervision

Level	Description of teacher	Description of supervisory role	Directive/ supportive behavior	Support function	Time period	Strategies
1. Intense Assistance: the goal of probationary supervision is to support the teacher in meeting the teaching standards of the school within a relatively short period of time or documenting a case for removing the teacher from the classroom. The meaningful learning of students is in jeopardy.	This level of supervision is reserved for the ineffective teacher who appears unable to improve without external intervention (1-2% of the population). The teacher does not have an internal locus of control and often externalizes responsibility for less than effective performance. An externally designed improvement plan is in effect and there is a strong likelihood of contract termination or non-renewal.	The role of the external supervisor is probably taken by the principal or assistant principal. There is a clear hierarchical learning relationship and status is not equal. There are frequent classroom observations and feedback conferences. While the improvement plan may be designed by the supervisor or jointly with the teacher, the responsibility for improvement is upon the teacher.	High directive behavior on the part of the supervisor.	Primarily evaluation and consultation.	Six to eight weeks.	Classroom observation, unit plan analysis and assessment analysis. Coupled with high quality feedback.

Level	Description of teacher	Description of supervisory role	Directive/supportive behavior	Support function	Time period	Strategies
2. Initial Direct Supervision: The goal of Initial Direct Supervision is to support the teacher in developing sufficient self-direction so that he or she can move to the Transitional Level and take responsibility for own learning.	Either a teacher new to the school or a young and inexperienced teacher. Approximately 10-15% of total population. Locus of control may be either internal or external.	Mentor: This role could be fulfilled by a principal, vice principal, head of department or team leader. While status is not equal, the mentor works to equalize it during the process. One of the goals of a mentoring relationship is collegial mutuality. The mentor diagnoses the needs of the mentee in respect to his or her development level and chooses congruent behavior. In this way the mentor also honors the experiences and strengths of the teacher.	Initially, high directive and high supportive behavior on the part of the Mentor. A high degree of guidance and direction is accompanied with encouragement and moral support. As the relationship develops over time, the degree of external direction becomes less.	Primarily consultancy, with minimal evaluation, and some coaching as appropriate.	12 months. All new teachers are expected to move from Initial Direct Supervision to Transitional Supervision within a 12 months period.	Classroom observation, unit plan analysis and assessment analysis, coupled with high quality feedback. Coaching used when appropriate.

Level	Description of teacher	Description of supervisory role	Directive/ supportive behavior	Support function	Time period	Strategies
3. Transitional: The goal of the Transitional Level is for the teacher to take full responsibility for his or her professional learning and ongoing improvement.	Most teachers, 50-70% of teachers in most schools. The assumption is that the teacher at the Transitional Level has internalized motivation and responsibility for professional learning, sets relevant and challenging goals, engages in honest and accurate self-assessment. The teacher at the Transitional Level tends to be a consumer of research information. There is an internal locus of control	Mediator of Adult Learning: The word 'mediator' is taken from our work in Cognitive Coaching. It refers to an individual who supports and facilitates the deep thinking of another person. The mediator withholds judgments, advice and recommendations and uses data and reflective questioning in order to locate and enhance the resources already present within the teacher. The mediator believes that the teacher has all the resources s/he needs in order to plan, reflect and problem resolve.	Low directive/ low supportive. The teacher is increasingly becoming a self-reliant achiever and does not need external direction. We see increased efficacy, flexibility, consciousness, craftsmanship and interdependence. The teacher is also in less need of external validation and encouragement.	Primarily coaching.	Ongoing.	Self-assessment, goal setting, structured reflective conversations, microteaching, peer coaching, structured and focused peer observation, book study groups, collaborative action research.

138

Level	Description of teacher	Description of supervisory role	Directive/ supportive behavior	Support function	Time period	Strategies
4. Leadership: The goal of the Leadership Level is to support the learning and growth of colleagues. It is essentially other-centered. The teacher has assumed responsibility not only for his/her own learning but also that of colleagues. This is a leader of adult learning.	The teacher at the leadership level tends to be actively engaged in sharing new knowledge and insights. This is the teacher who is pro-active about sharing articles, leading workshops, or facilitating collective inquiry. The Leadership Level teacher not only consumes new research and disseminates it, but also generates new knowledge through his or her action research. There is an internal locus of control.	Mediator of Adult Learning: The word 'mediator' is taken from our work in cognitive coaching. It refers to an individual who supports and facilitates the deep thinking of another person. The mediator withholds judgments, advice and recommendations and uses data and reflective questioning in order to locate and enhance the resources already present within the teacher. The mediator believes that the teacher has all the resources s/he needs in order to plan, reflect and problem resolve.	The mediator provides little or no direction. Instead, the mediator coaches the leadership level teacher to enhanced states of resourcefulness so that s/he is self-directed in planning, reflection and problem resolution.	Coaching.	Ongoing.	Self-assessment, goal setting, structured reflective conversations, microteaching, peer coaching, structured and focused peer observation, book study groups, collaborative action research.

In a Calibrating Conversation, the coach follows a five-step process:

1. Identify present level of performance and goal: The coach asks the teacher to identify the arena of the continuum (rubric) that the teacher would like the conversation to focus upon, identify the present level of performance and the desired level of development. The teacher selects the focus of the conversation – a critical dimension of self-direction – and then identifies the present level of performance (the self-assessment). The teacher then locates the desired level of development. For example, the conversation might go something like this:

Coach: You've been engaged in a self-assessment against the school's continuum of professional performance. Which dimension of the continuum would you like to focus upon today?

Teacher: I'd like to focus on my questioning skills. I'm a little concerned that I ask too many closed questions.

Coach: You're interested in exploring your use of questions to elicit student thinking. Reflecting on the different levels on the continuum, what are your thoughts about where your questioning skills might fall?

Teacher: I've looked over the continuum and I think my present performance is at level 2. I do ask some open-ended, really reflective questions, but I also ask a lot of closed questions. Level 2 suggests that open-ended, reflective questions are asked 'occasionally'. That's probably fairly accurate for me at the moment.

Coach: So you place yourself at level 2. Where would you like your skill level to be?

Teacher: Level 3 states that open-ended, reflective questions are asked regularly. I don't think I have the balance right. I want to get better at framing questions that cause students to think deeply and I want to ask them more frequently in class. I want to be at a level 3.

2. The coach explores with the teacher what might be some values and beliefs that underlie the desired level of development. This step in the conversation connects the goal with the teachers deeply-held belief system. It makes explicit why the goal is meaningful and galvanizes motivation. This is the step that provides coherence between external behaviors and internal values and beliefs. The conversation might go something like this:

Coach: The development of questions is clearly important to you. In what ways might improving your questioning skills be connected to your values and beliefs as a teacher?

Teacher: I really want students to think critically and independently. That's really important to me. That's a gift for a lifetime. Sure they need to learn content, but they also need to analyze, compare and evaluate – you know, higher order thinking skills. If I don't ask questions designed to elicit higher order thinking, students aren't likely to engage in it.

3. Identify possible strategies and support needed for reaching the desired level of development. This step in the conversation moves the goal (the desired level of achievement) from the theoretical to the operational. It asks the teacher to analyze and plan the learning process and to identify what specific resources he or she may require. The conversation might continue as follows:

Coach: You see a direct correlation between the questions you frame and the depth of student thinking. What strategies might you use to enhance your questioning skills?

Teacher: (Long pause). That's a good question. I usually just ask questions that come to me in the moment. I haven't actually thought about making questioning a part of my planning. (Another long pause). I mean it's sort of obvious now that I think about it. I can write a few open-ended, reflective questions as part of the planning process. Then I don't have to think of them on the spur of the moment. Actually, I need to think about what makes an effective, reflective question. What are the characteristics?

Coach: So one strategy you're exploring is to give yourself time in the planning process to craft questions designed to elicit deep student thought. Another strategy might to deconstruct really good questions. Beyond time, what other resources might be helpful in reaching your goal?

Teacher: I could probably use a model. I mean there are other people in my department. Sarah asks really good questions. I could ask her help. Better yet, I could ask to observe one of her classes and script her questions. I think she'd be OK with that.

4. Commit to application: This is the stage of the conversation where the plan becomes an immediate undertaking. The conversation might develop along the following lines:

Coach: So there are a number of resources and strategies that you are exploring. What next steps might you be taking?

Teacher: Well, I can ask Sarah to observe a class of hers. I can do that tomorrow morning.

Coach: You see Sarah as a very useful resource. What will you need to be mindful about in terms of building question design into your planning?

Teacher: Hmm. I guess I could make a note to myself, perhaps on the unit planner template itself. I could write at the top 'what good questions will I ask today?'

5. Reflect on the conversation: This is the metacognitive step in the conversation in which the coach asks the teacher to reflect on new insights or learnings that have emerged. The conversation might well follow in this way:

> **Coach:** You're planning to deliberately integrate question design into your planning. As you reflect on our conversation, what has been useful to you?

> **Teacher:** I hadn't thought about bringing questioning into the planning process. I just need to take a few minutes to frame some really good questions while I'm planning. Then I don't have to worry about ad-libbing them in the moment. That was really useful.

In closing

The improvement of the craft of teaching is contingent upon adult learning. There are different types of learning and there are different learner readiness levels. In terms of maximizing the learning experience for teachers, we need to design a system that allows (and compels) teachers to become architects of their own learning. They need to identify their own professional zone of proximal development, set for themselves challenging goals, devise strategies that will allow them to realize these goals, monitor process and reflect on the outcome. These are reasonable expectations.

References

Costa, A., Garmston, R. & Zimmerman, D. (2014). Cognitive Capital: Investing in teacher quality. New York: Teachers College Press.

Danielson, C. (2013). Framework for teaching evaluation instrument. Princeton NJ: The Danielson Group.

De Bono, E. (1992). I am right you are wrong: From this to the new renaissance: From rock logic to water logic. London: Penguin Books.

Drago-Seversen, E. (2009). Leading adult learning: Supporting adult learning in our schools. Thousand Oaks, CA: Corwin Press.

Doidge, N. (2007). The brain that changes itself: Stories of personal triumph from the frontiers of brain science. New York: Penguin.

Dweck, C. (2008). Mindset: A new psychology of success. New York: Ballantine Books.

Erikson, E. (1950). Childhood and Society. New York: W.W. Norton & Co. Inc.

Fullan, M. (2001). Leading in a culture of change. San Francisco: Jossey-Bass.

Garmston, R. & Wellman, B. (2009). The adaptive school: A sourcebook for developing collaborative groups. Norwood, MA: Christopher-Gordon Publishers.

Jackson, C. K. & Bruegmann, E. (2009). Teaching students and teaching each other: The importance of peer learning for teachers. Retrieved [12/12/14], from Cornell University, School of Industrial and Labor Relations site: http://digitalcommons.ilr.cornell.edu/workingpapers/77/

Kegan, R. (1982). The evolving self: Problem and process in human development. Cambridge, MA: Harvard University Press.

Next Frontier: Inclusion (2013). Towards inclusion: Planning our path. NFI.

Powell, W. & Kusuma-Powell, O. (2010). Becoming an emotionally intelligent teacher. Thousand Oaks, CA: Corwin.

Rooke, D. & Torbert W.R. (2005). "Seven transformations of leadership", Harvard Business Review, April 2005.

Chapter 8

It's all about reclaiming our profession

Sixty years ago, when Bill was entering primary school in Britain, the teacher was always right. She was the unquestioned authority. Even when she was wrong, she was right. Now, in many countries, the teacher is often perceived as always wrong. Neither of these perceptions is accurate or healthy.

The last several decades have seen a barrage of criticism leveled at teachers and at the teaching profession. This has been especially the case in the industrialized world – the United States, Britain and Australia. Some of the criticism is unquestionably warranted, but much of it has been spurious and even hypocritical.

Take for example Fox News' recent attack on Michigan teachers for their 'greed' and 'avarice' in seeking improvement in salary and benefits while in the same breath the same Fox News' commentators were defending the astronomical bonuses of Wall Street bankers! Or the constant refrain that teachers only work nine months a year and therefore have cushy jobs and don't really deserve a 'full time salary'. The latter comment is inevitably made by someone who has never been in the classroom as a teacher.

In some countries, it seems that the popular media has declared 'open season' on the teaching profession. In 2008 *Time* magazine ran a cover photograph of Michelle Rhees, the recently appointed Washington DC Chancellor of Schools, standing in a classroom, glaring at the camera while holding a broom. The title of the issue: 'How to fix America's schools … her battle against bad teachers.' More recently, *Time* magazine has again enraged teachers. Its 3rd November 2014 cover depicts an apple about to be crushed by a gavel with the title: 'Rotten Apples: It's nearly impossible to fire a bad teacher – Some tech billionaires may have found a way to change that.' The controversial *Time* cover sends several erroneous and pernicious messages.

First erroneous message: teachers are the primary problem in education. This assumes that there is a major problem in education and that teachers are the cause of it. This conveniently ignores socio-economic factors, school funding, the political landscape, and home environment.

Second message: There are lots of bad teachers – 'rotten apples'. There are unquestionably a few ineffective teachers and they do need to be removed from the classroom. Any system that protects ineffective teachers needs to be redesigned from the bottom up. However, are there really 'lots of bad teachers'? This doesn't align at all with our experience.

Applying leeches to anemic patients

Third message: Only business tycoons-cum-philanthropists like David Welch and Bill Gates can save education. Not only is this assertion unfounded, but also the manner in which the tech billionaires have gone about 'improving schools' has been counterproductive and has seriously damaged teacher morale and student learning. It can be likened to the well-intentioned arrogance with which 18th century doctors applied leeches to anemic patients.

Their highly funded initiatives have been all about identifying bad teachers and making the classroom and the curriculum 'teacher-proof'. This is both demeaning and demoralizing to the profession. As stated earlier in this book, improving schools is about teacher professional growth. Such growth occurs when we search for what is working well, analyze it, and replicate it. Teacher professional learning does not occur when we search for what is wrong in schools.

Politicians and the media have given enormous attention to the opinions of extremely wealthy individuals with no teaching experience, no pedagogical knowledge and no training in the cognitive development of children and have consistently ignored actual experts in the field. One of the reasons for this bias is that genuine experts in teaching and learning understand how complex teaching and learning actually are and they are not proposing simplistic 'silver bullet' solutions: smaller schools, more standardized testing, or merit pay for teachers.

Kathleen Harrison writes in her blog *Rethinking Education*:

> I get the feeling most people have no idea what goes into the work of which they are so critical... No CEO has a more complex assignment than that of a teacher – tasked with simultaneously meeting the individual and very different intellectual and social needs of dozens of students in a world demanding 21st century skills of its graduates. (07-11-2013)

The bad news for the quick-fix guys

For those who have never been on the inside of education, there is an enormous temptation to oversimplify schools and teaching. At the heart of much of the oversimplification is the reductionist idea, often brought in from the business community that success is monolithic and can be quantified. Success or failure in business can be neatly displayed on a balance sheet. Success in schools is certainly not monolithic and only certain aspects of it can be easily measured.

A hard fact that is often ignored by the quick fix-guys is that there is more that we don't know about teaching and learning than what we currently do know. That is what makes this a particularly exciting, stimulating and confusing time for teachers. We simply have more questions than answers. This is why teacher learning is so critical.

An alternative to hunkering down

Lest we think that teacher bashing is primarily an American pastime, Richard Gerver (2013), the former lead teacher at the Grange School in Derbyshire in the UK, writes:

> As a profession, we have become so battered by external forces that we have hunkered down in hope that the storm will pass; it is a natural instinct, when we are under pressure or threat, we retreat and seek a safer, simpler often-rose-colored shelter. (Leadership Teachers' Blog, *theguardian*, 26 June 2013)

The problem with this 'hunkered down' stance is that it negatively affects both student and teacher learning. We know from research in self-esteem theory that in school-aged children the relationship between self-concept (how we view our self) and success in school is *not* bi-directional. High self-esteem in no way guarantees academic success in schools. However, low self-esteem is directly and powerfully correlated to failure in schools. We believe that the same may be the case for teachers.

Social status and learning

Perceptions of social status and self-esteem affect learning. The groundbreaking research on the sociology of the classroom was spearheaded by Stanford professor Elizabeth Cohen and her colleague, Rachel Lotan (1997). For Cohen the classroom was a microcosm of society as a whole and students were perceived to occupy a hierarchy of status. In the classroom, classmates confer status on an individual on the basis of several criteria including academic success in school; physical attractiveness; interpersonal skills (popularity); and physical prowess (talent in sports).

Children with low status amongst their peers tend to be socially isolated and receive less teacher attention (Kusuma-Powell & Powell, 2015). In addition teacher expectations for low status children may be less demanding. Correspondingly, these children learn less than their high status peers. Cohen (1998) perceives student status in the classroom as malleable and that the teacher can serve to mediate student status.

Children (and adults) choose from whom they will learn and status plays a key role in the selection. We are much more likely to learn more from a high status individual than someone with low status. Mary Catherine Bateson (1994) points out that, in the 1950s, upper middle class British families often employed nannies to care for their children. The nannies usually came from the provinces – Wales, Scotland, or the south-west and had dramatically different accents than those of their employers. Without exception, the children did *not* pick up the accent of their nannies. Even very young children are sensitive to status and the role it plays in selecting who to learn from.

Like children, adult learning and professional effectiveness are affected by status. When a profession, such as teaching is perceived to have low status, it is accorded less respect and appreciation by the media, politicians and general public. Over time this scorn will take its toll on teacher morale and can result in the so-called 'self-fulfilling prophecy' in which we come to believe the perceptions and expectations of others.

Rediscovering professional eloquence

In 1990 Roland Barth wrote a now classic book entitled *Improving Schools from Within*, the major premise of which was that schools will not get better by external mandates or pernicious coercion. Schools can and will improve from within – by the individual and collective behaviors and decisions of teachers and school leaders. Barth (2006) perceives the most powerful predictor of high quality student learning in the classroom to be the quality of adult-to-adult relationships – relationships that revolve around mutual professional learning.

If we are going to reclaim our profession, what Richard Gerver refers to as 'rediscovering our professional eloquence' (2013), this process must begin by teacher self-directed learning in which we move individually and collectivity from accountability to internalized responsibility. Gerver writes:

> If we are to seize back our profession, our sanity and the rights of our kids, we must come out from the shelter and lead; we must stop simply reacting to the retro-thinking and endless baiting and start to fight back by demonstrating our vision in practice, we must demonstrate our professionalism and abilities to translate action research into active and organic teaching and learning.

The compelling vision for our schools is one in which teachers behave as responsible professionals; they design engaging, respectful and meaningful learning experiences for students not because they are forced or coerced to do so, but because they deeply value the learning of children. The compelling vision for schools is for teachers to become the architects of their own learning and build learning relationships with colleagues that translate into inspiring lessons for students. The compelling vision for our schools is for them to become truly communities of leaders of learning and for teachers to rediscover their professional eloquence.

References

Barth, R. (2006). 'Improving Relationships with the schoolhouse', Educational Leadership, March 2006, Volume 63, No. 6, p. 8-13, Alexandria, Va.: Association for Supervision and Curriculum Development.

Barth, R. (1990). Improving schools from within: Teachers, parents and principals can make the difference. San Francisco,: Jossey-Bass.

Bateson, M.C. (1994). Peripheral Visions: Learning along the way, New York, New York: Harpercollins.

Cohen, E. (1998). 'Making Cooperative Learning Equitable', Educational Leadership, September, 1998, Volume 56, No. 1, p. 18-21, Alexandria VA. Association for Supervision and Curriculum Development.

Cohen, E. & Lotan, R. (1997). Working for equity in heterogeneous classrooms: Sociological theory in action. New York: Teachers' College Press.

Gerver, R. (2013). 'Schools can handle change, but constant criticism has to stop', Leadership Teacher's Blog, The Guardian, 26 June, 2013.

Kusuma-Powell, O. & Powell, W. (in press). 'The changing face of learning support: The role of status in schools.' *Educational Leadership*, December 2015.

Other educational books by William Powell and Ochan Kusuma-Powell

Count Me In! Developing Inclusive International Schools, Office of Overseas Schools, US State Department

Making the Difference: Differentiation in International Schools, EAF Press, Kuala Lumpur, Malaysia

How to Teach Now: Five Keys to Personalized learning in the Global Classroom, Association for Curriculum Development and Supervision, Alexandria, VA.

Becoming an Emotional Intelligent Teacher, Corwin Press, Thousand Oaks, CA.

The OIQ Factor: How Schools can become cognitively, socially and emotionally smart, John Catt Educational, UK.

School Board Governance training: A Sourcebook of Case Studies (With Nicholas Bowley and Gail Schoppert) John Catt Educational, UK

By the Next Frontier: Inclusion

The Next Frontier Inclusion: A Practical Guide for International School Leaders, (with Kristen Pelletier and Kevin Bartlett and others) EAF Press, Kuala Lumpur, Malaysia

An Inclusive Toolkit (editors) EAF Press, Kuala Lumpur, Malaysia

Towards Inclusion: A Self Audit Protocol (with Kevin Bartlett and Kristen Pelletier) EAF Press, Kuala Lumpur.